"Over 80 percent of the patients chancing the physician's skills have little more wrong with them than what a considerate spouse, a kindly bartender, or a hefty raise in salary couldn't cure. Of the 20 percent left, most are amenable to the old tried and true workhorses: milk of magnesia, aspirin, an ice bag, or Preparation H . . ."

—Dr. Edgar Berman

A well-known physician, Dr. Berman has earned the right to use his spurs. A past president of MEDICO, a State Department and HEW consultant, he worked with Albert Schweitzer in Lambarene, was a pioneer in experimental heart transplantation, and has been a driving force in population control.

The Solid Gold Stethoscope

Warning: Your Doctor May Be
Hazardous to Your Health

Edgar Berman, M.D.

BALLANTINE BOOKS • NEW YORK

Disclaimer of Credit

Having turned a cold shoulder to *The Politician Primeval,* my ever-loving and loved wife, in her admirable consistency, did likewise to this ode to doctors. So in all honesty I am moved to reiterate my lack of indebtedness to her, directly or indirectly, for aiding, abetting, or even encouraging this latest venture.

Contents

Foreword

This is at once an outrageously funny and deeply depressing book. Dr. Edgar Berman takes a satirist's-eye view of his own medical profession, and finds it tragically and absurdly wanting. In chapter after chapter, dealing with various branches of the profession, he hilariously takes apart the competence, the commitment, and the ethos of the medical personnel. It is done with the swift, sharp, surgical scalpel of the satirist. The laughs are many, but the reader (and the patient) can say that it only hurts most when he laughs hardest.

It is a satirical book, done by a satirist. As one now more involved in politics than in medicine, I can testify to the author's satirical talents from having read his earlier book, *The Politician Primeval*. It drew blood. So does this book.

Dr. Berman underscores what many know from their own experience—the lost regard for medicine and for doctors on the part of the American people. Dr. Berman does not intend to castigate all doctors in the specialties he examines; there are good doctors in each. But the good practitioners—there are many, as I can testify from my own experience—are dragged down in public esteem along with their less competent and less scrupulous brothers. This book may seem to add to that loss of credibility by the profession. But a case can be made for a harsh, cleansing attack in order to prod the doctors into doing something about it.

ix

The causes for the loss of credibility of the medical profession lie very deep in the American society—in the growth of urbanization, in the rapid development of medical science and technology, in the tangle of specializations, in the metastasis of litigiousness on the part of patients, in the near disappearance of the old-time general physician. But most of all, they lie in the commercialization not only of medicine but of almost all the professions—the "bottom line" morality taken over from business enterprise.

The author speaks as one of them. He worked as a surgeon with Dr. Albert Schweitzer in Lambarene; he was one of the pioneers in experimental heart transplantation; he was a former president of Medico; he was a State Department and HEW consultant and a driving force in population control; more recently, he has been personal physician and adviser to a U.S. vice president. He has earned his spurs and earned the right to use them to goad his colleagues.

It follows that whatever housecleaning takes place will have to be done by the profession itself, in developing a new ethic—or returning to the old traditional one from which too many practitioners have departed. I trust this book can help in that direction by the satirical edge it gives to some home truths.

MAX LERNER

Preface

The Hypocritic Oath

I SWEAR by Midas, my malpractice insurance, the AMA, and all other of my gods and goddesses that according to my ambition and cupidity I will keep this Oath. I shall reckon him who taught me this art equally dear to me as my banker or broker, and relieve his necessities if required, but only if he shall relieve mine. I will impart a knowledge of this art to my own sons, if they accept amnesty and return from Canada and their communes. Bound by stipulation and oath according to the laws of the marketplace, I shall teach this art to none other, in order to keep the windfall within the family and medical establishment.

TO MINIMIZE competition from chiropractors, naturopaths, and Rosicrucians, I shall defame them in the finest tradition of my big brother, the medical society. I will follow any system and regimen laid down by any insurance company, public or private, filling out all forms as long as there is no limit on visits or laboratory tests, and no supervision by government snoopers. I shall fight to obstruct National Health Insurance (as I did Medicare) and contribute to the American Medical Association Political Action Committee (AMPAC) to further this. I consider all this necessary to maintain my income for the benefit of my demanding wife and my various monthly payments, not to mention my early retirement.

I SHALL abstain from every voluntary act of mischief or corruption, especially if there is the slightest risk of exposure. Nor will I prescribe uppers and downers to anyone not referred to me by a reliable source. In like manner, I will not give to a woman a pessary to produce abortion (when there are better, more legal and more lucrative ways of bringing this about).

I WILL pass my life and practice my art during my sober working hours but devote the rest of my time strictly to interest-bearing business, real estate, and other esoteric pleasures. I will not cut persons laboring under either a normal uterus or an enlarged tonsil. But for due and fixed consideration, in unmarked bills of low denomination, I will refer such cases to men who are regular practitioners of this work. In whatever houses I enter it will in no way be construed as solely for the benefit of the sick—for if they are ill enough they should come during regular office hours and thus disturb neither my rest, my hangovers, nor my golf handicap.

FURTHER, I shall neither commit nor condone seduction of females or males, especially if they are prepubertal, unless it is in strict accordance with the precepts of Masters and Johnson.

WHATEVER, IN my professional practice, I see or hear, I will not divulge except in the strict confines of the locker room, the bedroom, or in confidence to the grand jury. While I continue to keep this Oath unviolated may it be granted to me to enjoy my Chris-Craft, my Palm Beach condominium, and my tax write-off of trips both home and abroad, respected by all doctors in these times. But should I trespass or violate this Oath the reverse will surely be my lot— and a sad one at that.

1

The Sacred Saga:

From Purity to Curity to Security

For a physician as highly touted as Hippocrates, he pulled some boners he'll never live down. If this revered father of medicine were alive today and practiced what he preached, he'd be the only doctor in the world on welfare. Imagine such drivel as only "going into the house for the benefit of the sick," which went out with house calls, or "not to produce abortions," which was done in by the Supreme Court. And that snide, if necessary, "abstain from seduction of the female or male" (not only is it a definite interference with the rights of consenting adults, but sex is now an accepted psychiatric tool).

Yet none of medicine's great leaps forward would have been possible without geniuses like him. In the logic of diagnosis alone, even Jimmie the Greek must acknowledge the mastery of his ancient ancestor after reading the *Prognostications*. And in the art of medicine what contribution to the nobility of the profession can compare with the famous Oath now mumbled by every senior as his final farewell to ever opening a medical book again.

That Oath encompassed not only the obvious, like prosperity, but also the nebulous, like ethics, and held up for over 2,000 years. Though it doesn't keep the present medical gang strictly on the straight and narrow, it at least restrains them from running hog wild. The founding Greek did go a little too far with that one that goes, "With purity and holiness, I will pass my life

1

and practice my art." Just the first four words are enough to break up a grievance committee in the Bible Belt.

Nonetheless, this proud profession hasn't done badly. Though it begrudgingly admits that a running nose has stumped it for over five thousand years, any profession that can contribute so much to the sick and neurotic by the surgical lifting of the breasts and the chemical lifting of the spirit has come a long way. No doubt the common cold still niggles at their pride, yet they did stumble on the miracle of aspirin—though how it works is still a mystery to them. (It's hardly as therapeutic as the old Chinese elixir of buffalo dung and powdered dragon teeth, but it's a lot more palatable.)

God His Co-pirate

Until the most recent achievement of turning base patients into gold (the old alchemists' dream), the history of medicine was a partnership with God. It was a rare physician who made his deadly rounds without a word with his cosponsor. From Apollo the powerful, to Jesus the healer, no doctor in his right mind would have dared anoint a ripe chancre with yak fat and mare's urine until he had cleared it with the Almighty.

Ecclesiastic economists claim that at one time well over 70 percent of church income and attendance came via the medical route, most of it from prepaid solicitation of cures. But the new breed of scientist-healer substituted the saints and candles with miracle drugs and Valium to cure phlebitus and enuresis. Now, except at times of extreme unction or illness in his own family, no favors are asked or given. Even hospital chapels are now afforded less space than a linen closet and only those sure losers like the neurosurgeon are seen furtively coming and going.

Today it's strictly progress, innovation, and results —without the benefit of clergy. How can the prayers, amulets, and herbs of yesteryear compare with the modern up-to-the-minute copper bracelets, B_{12} shots, and Geritol. The enlightened patient will no longer be taken in by the primitive surgery of trephining the skull (boring a hole) to release the evil spirits when he can now have electric shock therapy that wipes out not only his present problems, but all memory of past troubles as well. Besides, the bruises and fractures heal readily and are not as painful as a hole in the head.

A Grave Business

This modern approach came about first by one of the great milestones of medicine. Some time around A.D. 900, the strangest curiosity developed among the healers—dallying about in the innards of their fellow men (living and dead) became fashionable in the trade. Grave robbery came into its own and soon became part of the internship. It did get out of hand for a century or two. When the demand got high and the price was right more and more bodies were brought in still warm to the touch. The law then had to tone down the exuberance of students dedicated to the pursuit of science.

The study of bones and bowels became a lucrative and respected adjunct to the preparation for a medical career. And once medicine could offer its initiates something more than incantations and aphrodisiacs to prescribe it became a serious pursuit for the profligate ne'er-do-wells from wealthy families. It was not as much fun as drinking or womanizing, but tracing the winding and twisting of thousands of arteries and nerves and memorizing other thousands of bones, muscles, and sinuses became a respectable sport. Peculiarly enough it surrounded those ancients with an aura of scholarship which elicited respect and admiration—and still does.

These dissections soon paid off. All sorts of symptoms were then assigned to different organs such as rage and anger to the spleen, vapors and faints to the liver or pancreas. This helped greatly in deciding whether to send an aging cardiac to the mountains or the seashore or whether to apply heat or ice to an injured part. It was much more precise and exacting than phrenology, or even those definitive instructions from Delphi.

The type of personality attracted to this calling responded then, as it does now, with the pomposity, overbearance and sense of infallibility necessary to intimidate and impress his patients.

Diagnostics I: How to Spot a Deadbeat

So medicine turned the corner; and, though cupping and animal sacrifices were not totally out, science was definitely in. But the big question was could it pay the rent?

Though the new methodology was important, the old meat-and-potato insider stuff on how to win influence and make a living was still very much alive. Those nonscientific tidbits of medical lore and experience were not lost and have been handed down to this very day. How else would a young doctor ever get to know the thoughtful demeanor, or the murmuring of unintelligible inanities when stuck for an answer on a tough case? How else would he learn the three signs and symptoms of a deadbeat and the two best ways to make him cough up or the ethical means of ditch-ing a patient without a lawsuit or even a grievance committee complaint; or the most subtle method of referring him to a colleague when he's broke or just about ready to cash in his chips?

The Deadly Sin: Imagination

Sir William Osler, another of the colossi of medicine, helped lay its more modern foundation. He gave the profession the word *Equanimitas*—which is etched on the medical brain like the Sermon on the Mount on the true believer's. In simple language it says, "never predict, say or put into writing to patient or colleague any more than you absolutely have to, or you'll regret it all the days of your professional life."

Another modern master, Freud, took the art a giant step further. His theory was that everything delicious, lascivious, and lecherous that we are luckily born for was the cause of most of man's physical and mental illness, second only to dear old Mom.

But none of these advances came easily. Men of vision who built a better mousetrap were viewed with suspicion by their colleagues—and rightly so, for a profession dealing in life and death could not allow itself to get bogged down in excesses of any kind, especially ethical or intellectual. Vesalius, the father of anatomy, was harassed to his dying day by his contemporaries for puttering around in freshly exhumed bodies without permission of the owner. Pasteur and Lister, as they described the microbe, were claimed to have spots before their eyes; and Freud was labeled a sex maniac. Today, the transplantation types like Barnard, Shumway, et al., waiting for the eyes, kidneys, and even the hearts of their fellow men (still warm in the body), are roundly condemned by their jealous fellow medicos.

One for Me, One for You,
and One for the Dermatologist Too

Like other professions, such as chiropractics or bail bonding, medicine has had its ups and downs and even rebellions (the AMA lost 70,000 paying members in ten years). Hippocrates himself caused one of the whoppers of all times when he wrote in his Oath, "I will not cut persons laboring under the stone, but will leave this to be done by men who are practitioners of the work." He opened the Pandora's box of specialization that has ever since spilled professional blood and guts onto the operating floor. The problem quietly festered until the Renaissance when the lowly barber surgeon used those words to rebel against his boss, the self-styled intellectual physician. It was really much ado about nothing then, for though their methods differed, the end results were always the same—both managed the utter depletion of the patient. One dehydrated his by purgings that could shrink a Sumo wrestler dry as a desert prune; the other, the barber, with lance and leech would bleach a ruddy Beef Eater a ghostly white, the envy of every Clorox ad.

After the longest internecine imbroglio on record, the surgeon finally became a specialist unto himself. The rift has never since been healed; they look down on each other and communicate only in the noble cause of making a living.

That was the beginning. The vying for patients and the gerrymandering of anatomy among the now innumerable specialties has spread far beyond the medical-surgical tiff. Their little Duchies are as well guarded and fought over as any predator's territory.

The general surgeon thinks the chest surgeon should stay away from the esophagus if the disease is near the diaphragm, and the head and neck man yield to no one if it's above the clavicle. The plastic surgeon thinks the nose and throat man should keep his fingers out of the nose and the general surgeon off the breast. The gynecologist fights the urologist for every bladder stone women can't pass and the proctologist proclaims eminent domain over the anus and rectum and is making nice inroads up the colon.

> Round and round the carping goes,
> Where it stops nobody knows.

Pioneer Medicine—150 Proof

Bringing it all up to date, we must give due credit to some of the great spontaneous movements which helped make medicine what it is today. Voodoo, that inheritance from fetish Africa and Creole Haiti, has now been sanitized to fit the culture of the day. The fun of chanting, shuffling, and chicken sacrifices cum orgies has been replaced by semi-civilized primal screams and group gropes, which may be just as much fun but yield far fewer cures than their predecessor.

Another proud page in the annals of medicine is the story of our own fearless pioneer physicians. Though untutored in the art and frequently not schooled at all, these brave, boozed souls have earned our nation's eternal gratitude. They roamed the pioneer trails, braving the elements and the scalpings along with the early settlers, and more frequently than not, resorted to their own elixirs to keep body and soul together. Their 150-proof medication, which is about all they had, assuaged the symptoms of practically any indisposition of young America, with almost no hangover.

They were all heart, those buckboard clinicians, their line of patter as convincing as any detail man's, and their product as comforting as bathtub gin. Proud but unprejudiced, they sold their medication to pioneer and red-skinned brethren alike. Their carefully distilled concoctions kept the iron-stomached pioneer feisty and the vulnerable savage loaded. It cost the Indians not only Manhattan, but more western real estate than the Homestead Act. On the negative side, it is also said to have fired up Sitting Bull to go scalp collecting at Little Big Horn.

In any event, our man with his "medicine" eventually helped win the west, and, with this proud heritage, we entered the new era of twentieth-century healing. This began auspiciously—sending our young scientists abroad—to Vienna—to learn the European ways. They returned to remove every tonsil, appendix, and uterus they could lay their hands on and also brought back the art of the couch, which they've never lived down.

Plug Him In and Make Him Well

In this historical process the patient also became educated. So today—unless things are up to the minute, like acupuncture or youthening shots—they just won't go for it. Even diagnostically they demand their money's worth, whereas their ancestors would have settled for the reading of dead chicken entrails to decide whether it was mononucleosis or hepatitis. A patient once satisfied to have his blood pressure checked and a stethescope put to his lungs, today won't budge unless every opening in his body is poked and probed by lighted tubes and catheters. If he doesn't get the full routine of being wired up so the voltage of brain, heart, and skin can be measured, he takes his body elsewhere.

So far it's been a grand saga; science against nature. In every instance the physician has comported himself (except at conventions and such) in a manner befitting his status. Now approaching the twenty-first century, the mind is boggled by lasers, computers, spare parts, and sex changes. This progress of medicine bodes a super-human as indestructible as the cockroach and as long lived as a Galapagos turtle, or—as we shall see later—as extinct as the Dodo.

2

The Poor Relations:
Patient vs. Doctor

Unlike many time-honored institutions such as usury, prostitution, and baseball, medicine has not suffered the ups and downs of a fickle following. The physician has always had the love and esteem of practically every patient—who lived to tell the tale. Win, lose, or draw, he's got a stranglehold on patients even Rasputin couldn't get on the tsarina—though it may be loosening.

The doctor-patient relationship, that mutual regard of healer and ailing, is one of the greatest stories ever told. Notwithstanding frequent blow-ups when a doctor refuses a night call, takes his phone off the hook, or cannot be reached on the golf course, there is still a strong link—not of forged steel but not of spit and string either. Even during those deadly courtroom confrontations in malpractice suits or compensation cases, the current of understanding still runs, though not as deeply as it used to. It's even more strained when the question arises about whether a gallbladder, stone for stone, could really be worth its weight in rubies. But if there is open hostility between the two, never let it be said that the profession lets on by even the lift of a medical eyebrow. That face is trained to go unruffled, come a slip of the tongue—or of the knife. Usually it's the lame, the halt and the hypochondriacal who blow it, by daring to question the doctor's proverbial infallibility.

The God-clod Connection

This once mutual affinity of the sufferer and the suffered is fabled in song and story from the time of the early Sumerian sorcerers to the charming give and take between Hollywood's Dr. Rubin and his wide, wide world who "always wanted to know . . . but were afraid to ask." Some say it's a kind of mutual hypnotism, like a python, and a rat, others, sort of a God-clod relationship. In any event, this staunch connection happened neither overnight nor by chance and has survived five thousand years of recorded history for good and deserving reasons.

First, those surviving through plague and war but unlucky enough not to bear up under the rigors of the leech, the purge, or the cardiac bypass were rendered uncomplaining by a peaceful, if well sodded, status. On the other hand, those who survive medicine are so ecstatic to find themselves still among the living they'd be pushing their luck for the next go round to knock the physician.

A customer knows, if Macy's doesn't have it, Gimbel's will. But if you've seen one doctor you've seen them all. The relationship seems separate but unequal with the doctor getting respect, adoration, and a handsome fee while the patient—if he's lucky—gets well. But who complains about a little inequality when that kidney stone is coming down the tube.

Las Vegas Arithmetic

There is also a certain arithmetic of illness going for this relationship—again mostly favoring the doctor. Over 80 percent of the patients chancing the physician's skills have little more wrong with them than what a considerate spouse, a kindly bartender, or a hefty raise in salary couldn't cure. Of the 20 percent left, most are amenable to the old tried and true work-horses: milk of magnesia, aspirin, an ice bag, or Preparation H. Some of the more chronic forms may need a little extra lift provided by Serutan ("natures" spelled backward), or even its social equivalent, gin.

Statistically the medical shaman starts way ahead of the game. He gets a lot of mileage in gratitude and even love out of diseases a Rosicrucian could alleviate. Little does the patient know that the few real diseases left over are now knocked out with a capsule or two. Not only does the doctor take full credit for those but his reputation isn't diminished by bread and butter surgical cinches. Cysts, warts, and hernias come complete with all of the OR trappings or bustling nurses, anesthesia, and gleaming cutlery. How could the patient feel anything but grateful and God fearing to come out of this nightmare alive, though it's about as risky as an FHA loan to Nelson Rockefeller?

Lay skeptics preach that the doctor-patient bond is frayed at the edges and ready for the dispose-all, and the doctor's attitude, "I'd better get paid before the stitches are out," doesn't help. But the real culprit in the fraying of the DPR is the efficiency expert. His "time is money" has converted this bond into a charming anachronism. The dawdling, coffee-drinking G.P. has been recycled. It happened when the computer found out that any time over nine minutes and thirty-three seconds spent with a patient is a bad investment. Every minute over that figure costs the average M.D. a minimum of 9 percent on the bank loan for his wife's new mink and the wall-to-wall carpet yet to be installed. How much rapport can be built up in a ten-minute contact in a cold cubicle, with a patient who's waited for four hours with no lunch and a doctor who has twenty more bodies to probe before dinner. Even to remember what each looked like last time around is a triumph in this revolving-door routine.

The Fast Physician Franchise

As the modern generation says, "Who needs it?" To them DPR is a drag, down the drain along with the friendly neighborhood butcher, baker, and candlestick maker. Medicine, like a fast-food franchise, must keep up with the times. House calls, family problems, and political discussions, all went out with F.D.R., the Hudson Super Six, and the zoot suit. Even the thorough chest tapping, pulse taking, physical examination is just a little too personal. The machine's the thing. That old-time "religion" can't compare with the surge of confidence and well-being that pervades the patient as he is bled, scanned, rayed, and wired up to every conceivable electronic device before he even sets eyes on his doctor. His sinuses may have long since drained themselves waiting for the appointment, yet he leaves the laboratory euphoric, if even confused as to which twin in the white coat was the doctor.

Medical automation also poses a psychological problem. Considering the inclination of patients to worship anyone (or -thing) they think helps them out of their misery, might there develop an "instrument-patient relationship"? It was always a calculated risk whether or not the patient would develop the same firm love and attachment to an electrocardiograph or a catheter. They do. Most patients with chronic illnesses would rather miss work than their treatment; tuberculars sometimes won't leave the hospital even when cured (see Thomas Mann's *The Magic Mountain*). There are many cases recorded of women yearning more for the romance of their cystoscopic treatment than for their husband's most prized possession.

The patient-doctor bond may not be what it used to be but the myth is too good a thing to let go. If the image of the profession is a combination of guardian angel, haven of succor, and last stop before the freeway, the AMA isn't going to let it disappear into thin air even though they know that this false sense of security may disappear after the first nonanswered night call.

Don't Be Half Safe

To keep the patient hooked, the profession still resorts to a few tried and true ruses. Is it by chance that a bare few of 300,000 physicians can write anything but graffiti on a prescription pad? Also when they do so well on talk shows why are they stricken with full-blown autism when it comes to explaining what the X ray shows or what went wrong? Long ago Aesculapius said that the more a patient knows the less confidence he has. What better way to prevent snoopers from digging up some of the grave errors.

If the DPR is ever laid to rest it won't go out with a whimper. As the AMA puts it, it's as American as the Constitution—and not to be tampered with. The DPR is a shining example of the American way of free enterprise. Physician groups testifying against National Health Insurance at congressional hearings hail the old DPR as a symbol—sacred as Mother's Day—and as the only sure means to save our country from the ravages of socialism (just as they did against Medicare—don't they ever learn from their mistakes?). Stars with megapractices like DeBakey and Christiaan Barnard who can't remember many of the faces much less the names of their patients (unless they've been on a coin or the cover of *People* magazine) swear by the DPR.

At least as far as the profession's concerned, the myth of the DPR has been more valuable than beads and fire water to keep the natives restful. Whatever else in medicine may pass away, the rod and the staff, with serpents entwined, will comfort the sick and neurotic all the days of their lives. And yea though they both walk through the shadow of the valley of death, the M.D. should fear no evil (except malpractice) and the patient may take solace in the dedication of his healer—or the peace of the hereafter, whichever comes first.

No matter the circumstances, doctors will always have deep faith in their own image—the image of the Father, the Son, and the Holy Ghost. As for the patient, he is only the true believer. Isn't that what the relationship is all about?

3

Bad Medicine:
The Pathetics of Ethics

Show me a physician in the slammer and I'll show you an impostor, a maverick, or one who did his wife in, in cold blood. Show me a doctor censured by the County Society and I'll show you one who hasn't paid his AMA dues. This is an unbelievable record. Politicians of all shades and affiliations from governors to precinct captains are behind bars; the legal profession from judges like Kerner to attorney generals like John Mitchell to vice-presidents like Agnew are well represented on the dockets of grand juries; executives of multinational corporations regularly pay their price-fixing fines; mineworker officials and shop stewards are sentenced for arson, booby trapping and contracts (not the wage-hour kind). But not the doctor. He's cleaner than a toothed forceps right out of the autoclave. He's got ethics.

No matter the rumors of fee gouging, tax evasion, or unnecessary operations, it's the rare M.D. that doesn't do it ethically. Even with narcotics, only an uneducated layman like the district attorney would wonder what kind of terminal cholera could demand tincture of opium by the bucketful or what range of obesity demands amphetamines in shopping bags. Sooner or later the public and the courts must realize that disease is only in the eye of the physician. There are some miscarriages of justice such as Dr. Max Jacobson (Dr. Feelgood) in New York who is in very deep trouble for keeping the high and mighty (including some presidents and their men) higher than mighty with his upper shots. Though it's been shown he bought and used 700,365 needles from 1964 through 1972, the Regents are still undecided about censuring him.

Even when caught red-handed by sneaky vice squad cops posing as patients (a tactic which just indicted a prominent Maryland chief of surgery—though he was later acquitted after a change of venue), the authorities better remember that only a physician's word can implicate another physician. And the chance of a doctor squealing on one of his colleagues is about as great as a Sicilian fruit vendor ratting on the Godfather.

Unethics Reduces the Caduceus

The good name of medicine goes back to the beginning, when dealing with life and death demanded standards of conduct and dedication of almost papal sanctity (though even some of the Holy Fathers got caught selling indulgences or anything else not nailed down in the Vatican). Today, in the same tradition, the profession is indefatigable in policing itself, though some prosecuting attorneys, with their suspicious minds, seem to feel that many a grand jury is denied its rightful quarry.

There are, no doubt, some collective instances of behavior which could be deemed unethical, such as the recent strike of doctors in San Francisco and New York because of exorbitant malpractice premiums. But what institution can pay its bills by treating only emergencies? The strange thing about this strike is that though only 15 percent of the hospital beds were used, there was no great suffering or increase in mortality. Another instance may be the bit of overcharge in the methodone clinics. In New York, under Medicaid, Dr. William A. Triebel, a psychiatrist, was paid

$857,500 for his year's work (in his spare time) while some of his colleagues were doing the same job for as little as $668,000 and one even at $221,000 working only two or three days a week. They maintain that even at those prices "it's hard to make ends meet."

Though some of the more minor issues—like physician dope addicts in the operating room, cash before cut, converting a human into a zucchini by psychosurgery are not exactly top priority in the policing department, the AMA earns its keep where it really counts, with issues like doctor advertising.

Blazing Shingles

Though not many doctors have heard of it, the AMA's gospel, "The Principles of Medical Ethics," is very big on the advertising thing. Only thanks to this does one not see demeaning ads in the Sunday *Times* blazoning, "You all come on down to Texas for Professor Quickfinger's new heart operation." Never! The eyes of Texas (and the AMA) are upon them. It's only in the course of public service or education that the good doctor is seen by ten million potential patients on the *Today,* the *Tonight,* and the *Tomorrow* shows— singing along with Mitch, clowning along with Johnny Carson, or playing straight man to Dean Martin. Anyway, only the few at the top are invited to these educational programs.

The diet supersalesman, like the most reputable doctors Atkins, (the late) Stillman, and Solomon (this last, after trimming the fat off the governor, became Maryland's Secretary of Health), stick strictly to the letter of the ethical code. No thirty-second spots, no classified ads, no billboards for them. Their publishers may write discreet blurbs for their books such as "shed pounds with Dr. Stillman's Ice Cream and Matzoh Ball Diet," but nothing garish or demeaning to the profession. These nutrition experts are solely interested in a fat free (if dollar foolish) America. If it takes a few radio and TV "educational" talk shows guaranteed to take off the pounds and help the heart—God bless those ethical gentlemen. If in the slimming process they develop a best seller and their practices fatten—so be it.

To facilitate any ethical physicians in educating America toward a more health conscious existence there is a P.R. specialist, Joyce Hauser, ready in the wings. She can get anyone with an M.D. degree on prime time if they have the professional prerequisites of having acupunctured a thousand patients with tired blood (after the necessary weekend training in Hong Kong), implanted hair plugs in Frank Sinatra, or erased eye bags from Senator Proxmire.

The medical society watchdogs in each state know what's important. They may overlook a shot doctor like Jake the injector to keep the jet setters like J.F.K. or Ari O. on a perpetual high, they may even look the other way when the little ole family doc helps the juvenile with a snort or two. But they are not about to ease up on the Madison Avenue type of unethical practice.

Psst! Need an Abortion Cheap?

For instance, they were right on the ball when a board-certified gynecologist in New York and his qualified assistants were found soliciting at every airport terminal as soon as the abortion laws were liberalized. Though only one of many, he was caught redhanded and they weren't about to let him off the hook. They made an example of him as a warning to other unethicals, according to Dr. Lawrence Essenson, chairman of the Board of Censors of the medical society of the county. They threw the book at this cheap fetus chaser who would besmirch the good name of an entire profession for a few paltry bucks. He received a full one-page letter on official state society stationery, delineating his activity (entirely private, of course) in an almost condemnatory fashion. Its effect was immediate. This miscreant felt so discredited in the eyes of his fellow doctors that he wasn't seen in an airport for two weeks.

There are few others in the whole profession so well reprimanded for stumbling off the beaten path, certainly not those who accept fees for testimonials on anything from golf clubs to baby food. For instance, the only gripe that could come from organized medicine against that Burt Reynolds of the profession, Dr. Paul Keith of Venice, California, who was the nude centerfold in *Playgirl,* would have been for selling himself so cheap. Imagine any self-respecting doctor wasting a whole day for a measly one thou, when he could have done better with Medicaid. If the profession decides to bring a case against him, it will probably be referred to the psychiatric section for showing delusions of candor.

As we can see, flouting of the ethical concept is not taken lightly by the powers that be. But there is a limit to punishing a fellow healer. According to Dr. Edwin J. Holman, secretary of the AMA's Judicial Council, no doctor has as yet been suspended or had his state license revoked for grave offenses of this nature—in the past twenty years. If the societies' higher councils tend to take draconian measures with that wayward nurse who does an occasional D and C on the kitchen table, they tend to temper justice for their own colleagues with their natural and understandable mercy.

Despite all of the rigid self-policing there is an occasional slip-up. In these medical miscarriages, a physician might find himself standing before the bar in the court of law. But like a man, he takes his lumps just like any other citizen. No quarter is asked but, it must be admitted, some is given. The coincidence that some 60–80 percent of all cases tried in court demand a medical consultant and that the most lucrative cases need the advice, council, and testimony of the friendly specialist has nothing to do with the court's leniency toward physicians. But still a medical degree is never worth more than two Louis Nizers and one fixed judge.

But at worst, what kind of crimes can a doctor perpetrate? Is a little padding of the Medicare bill, a tax amnesia, or leaving a small tool in a patient's innards so earthshaking as to demand the incarceration of men preoccupied in the service of society? Even those all too frequent murders of wives by doctor spouses is excused as a product of the constant emotional turmoil of life-and-death decision making. (Ironically Dr. Sheppard, whose murder accusation gave the profession the blackest eye, was merely an osteopath.)

The 18 kt, Chris-crafted, 7-handicap Spartan

One of the more unfair ethical accusations, always alluded to by the press is the canard that doctors are money grubbers. Though like any other corporate executive a shingle on the wall rates a Royce with his Roll, this calumny couldn't be further from the truth. Most patients understand that the self-denial of those long years of expensive training, office furnishings, and computers (some costing $50,000) doesn't come from peanuts. Even then, scraping along in terms of condominium survival is only the bare necessity for good practice. The paneled wall, the lush carpet, the uniformed receptionist and nurses, not to mention club memberships, professional travels (to keep up scientifically) are all measures taken ultimately for the good of the patient. The modern patient needs the sweet smell of success, as much as he needs a placebo or a B^{12} shot. It builds confidence and trust. As the psychiatrists say about cash on the barrelhead—it's part of the treatment.

If the truth be known, even the robber barons of this art lead a rather spartan existence. What's left after the mortgage, private school tuitions, Super Bowl tickets, and other bare creature comforts are paid for? And as to that perennial gripe about the Mercedes and Ferraris, would the mother of a desperately sick child question the necessity for 400 horsepower under the hood to speed that angel of mercy on his lifesaving mission? No, it cannot be proved—at least not beyond a shadow of a doubt—that the worship of the almighty dollar has in any way sullied the dedication of the almighty doctor.

These are the real gut issues that grievance and ethics committees all over the world are plagued with but as shown, doctors themselves do a mighty job in keeping the profession on the straight and narrow with the health of the patient ever in mind.

The Ashcan School of Surgery

Other than little human failings like operating on the wrong patient, sending the other woman's baby home with mother, or connecting the anesthesia mask to a lethal gas instead of oxygen (which are all within the margin of human error), there is another sore spot with the profession that is constantly rubbed raw by the press. It's that old unnecessary-operation bugaboo. So a Medicaid patient is operated on 236 percent more than the average—what difference, the government pays. Frequently it's brought out in the open by those holier-than-thou, full-time, university types who get their salary whether they ever see a patient or have to meet the monthly nut. It's easy for a John Knowles to "tell it all" from the throne room of his Mass. General Ivory Tower—just before heading up the Rockefeller Platinum Tower. Did any of those Mayo or Crile clinic establishment types ever have to struggle to make a windfall buck to keep body and soul together?

The question boils down to: Are a few normal organs in the ashcan worth all the fuss and excitement? Aren't most of those tonsils and ovaries expendable? Aren't there hospital tissue committees (of friendly colleagues) that are keeping tabs, ready to censure if the surgeon goes over his quota of normal gallbladders for the month?

As the doctors have always seen it if they can't be trusted with matters of ethics, who can? The matter of kickbacks, money grubbing, or advertising has been handled very neatly for centuries, why rock the boat now with grand juries and such? Even euthanasia can be managed by the profession. If a doctor knows when to open a boil or give digitalis to keep the ticker pumping, shouldn't he be trusted to put someone out of his misery—as long as it isn't someone near and dear to him? How can the Holy Father and the Right to Lifers know whether a one-inch blob of jellylike stuff in the womb has life or not? The Pope didn't argue when his doctor told him his prostate needed massage.

The Best Things in Life Are Free

But the old order changeth and what's illegal and wrong today is legal and gone tomorrow. There are hundreds of caveats that have already gone the way of all ethics. Abortions which used to be loudly condemned and quietly circumvented are not only legal now, but a great little income producer.

Also, in this day of equal opportunity, that ancient

enshrined fee-splitting science has now gained respectability—if not the actual seal of approval. In this age of medical economics, why should the referring physician be discriminated against, especially when the highly paid specialists are more than willing to share with their less fortunate colleagues, or with lawyers for that matter? As with lawyers, a slice of the patient pie, so to speak, keeps everybody happy, and if the IRS doesn't blow the whistle, why should the AMA? Would any right-thinking medical doctor refer a patient for an operation just to share in the loot (unless there was an unusually large margin call or a similar type of emergency)? It's really much ado about little and something physicians are too sensitive about. Actually the controversy itself doesn't hurt. It gives the public the feeling that the profession is really concerned.

Doctor knows best. The full force of the profession will never falter in saving life and limb. In the crunch, saving neck (their own) is even better and the medical banner will ever remain unsoiled. So far self-policing has worked like a charm, so who needs the interference of a prying public and a probing government when all's right in the best of all possible worlds?

To medicate the words of the immortal bard, he who steals my purse, steals cash; but he who filches from me my good name—steals my credit cards.

4

The Patient Patient:
Bloody but Unboweled

Observing the doctor-patient ecology in its natural bed, couch, and clinic habitat there's no doubt that as the sick need the doctor, so the doctors need the sick. How else could the profession experiment with new drugs, practice new operations, and gather statistics? Where could the physician get grist for the mill of teaching interns and medical students? Individual patients may be expendable but as a group they're as indispensable to doctors as the insurance form they come with. To understand the doctor without knowing the patient is like trying to comprehend a New Guinea cannibal without knowing his dietary habits. To be at the beck and call of a sick body and mind and keep an even keel takes either an uncommon strength of character or an incurable mental weakness. Since the former is not common in the profession, one must sympathize with the doctor's lack of sympathy with the frailties and demands of the unhealthy and his frustration at knowing they are his only source of income.

The profile of the thin-blooded American patient is blurred unless one takes into account his humble beginning. As Darwin showed back in the forest primeval, the present-day incumbent of a bed in the Mayo Clinic was a titmouse with shingles or a hyena with hemorrhoids. The ailing weren't born yesterday. Patients get their gallbladder stones or other sicknesses programmed in their genes just as they get their personality or their talent. The Rolaid-consuming executive has his ulcer as a hand-me-down from the skull-cracking, on-the-go Neanderthal. That housewife with her monthly irregularity got it naturally from that Cro-Magnon cavewoman scared witless and menstrualless by the sight of a hungry wolf dragging off one of her litter.

But whatever they have and however they got it, today they're no longer content with licking their own wounds. They want it done for them and there's only one legal wound licker—the doctor. Now, through the courtesy of Blue Cross, Medicaid and Medicare, it's "sick or not, we're here"—to be licked six hundred million times a year. With that great omnibus health insurance carrying all and sundry, more and more roads lead to—the waiting room. They converge in droves, demanding their pound of consolation, conversation, or, occasionally, relief and cure—if there is anything to relieve or cure. Still they come. At those prices who cares?

The Whiplash Retirement Plan

It's an ill disease that doesn't blow somebody some good and if the patient is on the alert he can cash in on some golden opportunities. Today the whiplash is more of an annuity than a spinal condition. Medicare takes on the aura of a weekly senior citizens picnic on the cool green lawn of a waiting-room carpet. Blue Cross is a package deal at charter rates (double occupancy only). It's become more popular than weight-watching spas, Borscht Belt weekends, and Caribbean cruises. Why not? Two weeks off with pay, breakfast in bed, daily massage, and service at the touch of the bell. It beats most Holiday Inns—and it's free. With a little bit of luck and major medical there is that added luxury even the Shah of Iran couldn't refuse—intensive care.

Those still on their feet settle for office visits and seem to get great satisfaction from every new gimmick the medical journals dredge up. There's one born every minute for ear staples or just routine placebos. Try to convince the Linus Pauling vitamin fanatics that a crate of oranges a day doesn't keep the sniffles away. A splash of Sunday morning holy water does as much good. But any group of people spending $300 million a year in laxatives can't be all wrong.

The Practice Called Mal

Being exposed to these medical whims and fancies, it must be comforting for the patient to know that if everything doesn't go just so—it may be very rewarding. This brings up something near and dear to the modern patient's heart—as it strikes fear and loathing in the physician's—malpractice. Though fast becoming a household word, malpractice has been so demeaned and misinterpreted by the doctor that even the good it does goes unnoticed. To the patient it's like a lottery. You put a little premium on the line and if lady luck, a shrewd lawyer, or a generous jury smiles on you, Bingo! You've got it made. It's part and parcel of an $8-billion democratic system with liberty and luxury for all. More important, in his simple little way, it's the patient's only means to get even against overwhelming odds.

Thirty years ago, suing a surgeon for amputating the wrong leg or taking out the good kidney was unimaginable. The patient bore it like a good soldier with a stiff upper lip. But now the new patient breed knows that its medical hope is bored stiff with the same old aches and pains and the sights, smells, and sounds of their predispositions and indispositions. That far-off look in the doctor's eye as he taps and probes is a dead giveaway; mentally, he's out on a smooth green fairway while visions of golf balls dance in his head. It's small wonder the surgeon remembers what to operate on, much less worry about which side. But what irks the patient is not so much the lack of explanation or apology for the missing member, whether leg or kidney (though it does pose problems when the other one's remaining days are numbered), it's the above-it-all look on the doctor's face while getting paid handsomely to boot.

It's all wrong to think, because of the malpractice bugaboo, that patients are more mercenary than the average consumer. They may want a little extra for the inconvenience of a lifetime in a wheelchair or a wasted day hooked up to an artificial kidney, but, psychologically, getting even is most important. They all know their insured rights, and sooner or later their gorge also rises. Being given the bum's rush is galling. Being whisked out without even a little give and take or a Polish joke or two is an indifference they won't put up with. Patients aren't unreasonable. They don't even insist on cures. They only want survival in the manner to which they have become accustomed, with a word or two of encouragement. They frankly admit that the receptionist or nurse gives unstintingly of her time (and even an occasional diagnosis or prescription) but if they're paying for a $75,000-a-year man, why settle for a $9,000-a-year girl?

So it's not all one-sided. Patients are getting a bad name just because they haul doctors into court 1600 percent more than they did ten years ago. Doctors are up in arms with devastating strikes and slowdowns (carefully scheduled only during tennis weather). Yet as the doctor passes it on to the patient, it's the doctor who complains. The patient, on the other hand, takes it like a man, maybe shelling out a little more in premiums—but knowing that the rewards will be more than generous.

If the thought of malpractice grates on a surgeon's

nerves and makes his hands shake he could be doing both himself and his patients a favor by meeting with them halfway. If he would spend as much time with his patients as he does with the detail man he might be able to restrain some of the skyrocketing malpractice premiums. A little small talk, nothing incriminating or even revealing, would go a long way. Not that patients wouldn't still sue, expose, and maliciously gossip—but it would be more amicable and maybe they'd settle for less.

Just listening might be the straw that would break the malpractice back. Do Rosicrucians or naturopaths have to pay out as much as $42,000 in malpractice premiums every year, like some New York doctors? They listen. Do Christian Science Readers, whose cure rate is at least as good as the neurosurgeons', worry about being hauled into court? No. They listen. And the biggest rub—lawyers are the best listeners of all.

Dr. Jekyll Hides His Spleen

Though most patients show no ill will against the doctor, there is a lot of hostility bottled up. Sure it's love and respect when the throat is strepped and the temperature soars; then their savior with his mirrored halo, his probing scepter, and his capsuled manna can do no wrong. But when the temperature is again simmering below 98.6 and the spots are gone, the bad mouthers are at it hammer and tongue. The doctor doesn't just take these jibes and slurs and roll over in a dignified doctorish way.

Patients would never believe the spleen the modern Dr. Jekyll hides. Let them get a load of that good samaritan at the end of a seven-hour operation and catch the jaundice tainting the pure white sclera of that kindly eye. The benign façade of compassion is

stripped away only when the patient is safely anesthetized or unconscious. Only then does the leer appear;
only then does the doctor mock the patient's complaints
or repeat (in dialect) his begging for a shot with the
nurses and interns rolling in the OR aisles. The faithful
would never believe the snide ribaldry in the whispered
consultation of the silver-headed experts.

A Crock Is Not a Pot

The general term used universally by physicians for
the ill or not so ill is "crock." There is a "crock who
complains too much or not enough"; a "crock who's
sick too much or not enough"; or "one who camps on
his doorstep too much or not enough." This endearing
term has Nordic and ancient English roots meaning an
old barren ewe or a decrepit horse. Even then, it
doesn't begin to convey the depth of the doctor's real
feelings, which, as said, he hides so well from his un-
anesthetized meal ticket.

The doctor's orderly mind honed to a blunted edge
by memorizing the 5,000 Latin parts of the human
anatomy (remembering only the important ones like
tonsils, gallbladder, and appendix) has a need to
classify everything, especially his big problem—the
patient. Diagnosis and treatment are a cinch. Most
diseases are hard to miss. But putting up with the different types of loony behavior shown by the average
patient is something else.

Disease has different effects on different types. For
instance, pain usually turns captains of industry into
blithering jellyfish. Two minutes with a rolling stone
(kidney, that is) would convert a Joe Namath type
into a simpering eunuch begging the medical plumber
to ram a foot-long steel tube up his most prized parts.
On the other hand, a little thyroid condition could

turn the pink powdered Helen Gurley Brown female into a riproaring sign-carrying Germaine Greer. If the basic personality can be pigeonholed, the doctor doesn't have to worry about the disease. He then immediately has the upper hand—which is crucial for any doctor-patient relationship.

Number 1: The Bread and Butter Crock

Number 1 in any patient pigeonhole is the B & B (bread and butter) Crock. Those same nine-out-of-ten TV doctors who always agreed that Dristan drains all five sinuses would also pick the B & B Crock as leading all the rest to their doors. He makes up the bulk of the 80 percent who are not only free from fevers (though hardly from fervors) but also from microbes, warts, or failing organs. These happy hang-ups with their vague symptoms are as uncontaminated by disease as if they'd been autoclaved at 5,000 degrees like operating room linen. These charmers mainly come in two complementary neurotic packages: male and female.

The Screw

The female patients—whether pampered housewife, harried Madison Avenue account executive, or Russian shot putter—have for some reason the same underlying etiology. It's called male (especially the subculture husband). They live with him, put up with him but know in their hearts they should have run off with Robert Redford when they had a chance, before being pregnantly decorated with hemorrhoids and chevroned with varicose veins. These beauties come to the physician drippingly fat (but never eat a thing); are rarely out of the sack by noon (but never sleep a wink), and are stimulated to erotic delight by *Deep Throat* (but are taken with splitting migraine as soon as they hit the connubial mattress). Their symptoms are about as nailable as a UFO, "I hurt all over, inside and out." Unluckily the cure for those legions of the battered wife syndrome is never permanent, for they have but one uterus to give to their neurosis.

The Nut

On the other end of the seesaw is that dominant, take-over breed of alley-cat husband who made her what she is today and whose totality of complaints come from guess who. His symptoms start in the early morning when he has dire nausea at first sight of that frowsy early morning eyeopener. He has a partial remission during the day but an exacerbation building up to a 3-martini zinger when he has to face up to his evening homecoming. Still, he is a responsible family man who has a chronic priapism for that platform-shod, gumchewing, floozy of a receptionist but suffers a wet-wash limpness in the marital bed. His giveaway symptoms center on his bowel movements, his chronic fatigue, and his postnasal drip. Any second-year medical student could tell him his problems—but, that's the one thing he doesn't want to hear. He's actually not too unhappy with them.

Number 2: The Gleaners and Die-ers

Most patients come to a doctor with one common denominator—not the fear of flying—but dying. They glean death from every little symptom. The first sign of swelling, it's cancer; a cough is Miner's Lung; pain down the arm, no question; and hemorrhoids, the first step to a colostomy. These mountain/mole hillers are not hypochondriacs, for they know they're beyond the help of medication. Every sneeze is one slide nearer the grave and every degree of temperature is some lethal tropical illness, caught in the rain forests of Palm Beach. They usually live to a ripe old age.

Number 3: The Shopper Crock

This crock has visited every doctor he can squeeze into his tight schedule and is satisfied with every one of them until a new one comes along. He's always on the alert for that fresh medical face across town or that intern (with the light touch) who just finished his weekend course at Mayo's. All are temporary miracle workers. These crocks are in constant motion—seeking their medical messiahs, whom they hope they'll never find.

Number 4: The Reluctant Crock

This type goes pale if he should by accident pass a doctor's shingle. Better a black cat than a white coat cross his path. To him M.D. means "medical death." Only as a last resort does he come face to face with the un-maker, usually in the emergency room, toes up. He knows that time is a great healer and that the lump, the boil, the bloody discharge, or that squeezing pain in his chest will go away any minute. He is microphobic, polishes every doorknob and washes his fried chicken finger-licking pure before he'll have a barrel of fun. When he finally gives in, it's a tossup whether he belongs to a hospital or to an enbalmer.

Number 5: Practitioner Without a License

This one will not only take every drug, potion, massage, enema, or inunction that he can lay his hands on (without a prescription) but knows at the first sign of an indisposition what combination and what sequence to use them in. He can't wait to get sick to test his diagnostic and therapeutic acumen. He's the type that would be ready to operate on himself with mirrors and instructions by radio if taken with an attack of appendicitis in a submarine under the South Pole. He's been known to stagger out half dead rather than be in the hands of a doctor who knows less than he does (and there are some). He's also part Shopper Crock.

Number 6: The Specialist Crock

To him, the family doctor never was. Not going to a specialist right off (without the middle man) is risking life and limb. If the exact sub-sub specialist isn't contacted with the first rash, pain, or palpitation, it may be too late.

On the first visit he inspects the parchments from high school to the board specialization. In case of emergency, around his neck, along with his blood group, is a tag with a list of ultra specialists for every sign and symptom. Rarely does his family or circle of friends suffer under the blade or the scope until a confusing parade of prima donnas belly-up bedside to preside over their special pound of flesh. No groan is left unheard, and no specialist left unturned.

Number 7: The Leechy Nut

This patient is forever. Any halfway kind word murmured under the breath by a doctor in a moment of weakness or just one lucky treatment, and he leeches on till death do they part. He can't be shaken off by insults, hours of waiting, overcharging, complications, or outright malpractice. And that's not the worst of it: he brings his sisters and his cousins and his aunts—all the same type.

Jesus at Calvary should only have gotten such adoration from his disciples. The doctor botches a vein with a purplish bruise the size of a hen egg—the patient apologizes. The M.D. is a half-day late to the office (from the club), and the patient bemoans taking up his precious time. She even lets the important patients in ahead of her without a murmur. When she gets a complication she is ashamed to return for follow-up because she caused him so much trouble. She is no Shopper Crock.

Number 8: The Chip Off the Old Crock

The chip is mainly on the shoulder and is easily jostled. When the nurse asks the Chip for his complaint he lifts an eyebrow: "That's for me to know and you to find out" or, better, "What am I paying you for?" He compares treatments, the number of tests, X rays and cardiograms he gets per visit with other patients as if he were coin collecting. At the hint of a slip-up he is on the phone to the medical society, the AMA grievance committee, and Ralph Nader. He complains if the magazines aren't up to the minute or the Muzak doesn't feature Sinatra. He calls the doctor at any time, day or night, at his own convenience and insists on being seen for his lower-back pain ahead of the patient with cardiac arrest but pays his bill only after much haggling and the third notice from the collecting agency. Unlike the rare decent patient who waits his turn, uncomplainingly pays his bills, and gets every complication in the books, this one sails through a heart transplant as if it were a tetanus booster.

Number 9: The Convivial Crock

These are hale fellows well met, who'd rather spend time in a waiting room than a board room or a dining room. They are frequently senior citizens, but not always. As a group their illnesses are purely an excuse to meet regularly at specified times for their Medicare hour in the waiting room. The only thing missing at the weekly gatherings are agendas, guest speakers, and adjournment with a rousing God Bless America. The chronics among them are sought out by their patient peers for the last word in "doctor talk," having had their disease the longest and seen the largest array of doctors. They trade symptoms as if they were wives, the most exotic or the most miserable being given their due respect. The *Guinness Book of Records* could tap this as a rich resource for details of un-interrupted weeks of constipation or number of nightly bathroom sallies. These people don't care how late the doctor is, or even if he shows up at all.

So this is the patient, sick in mind or body or both. All that can be said when stacking him up against the doctor is that they deserve each other.

5

The G.P.:

General Paralysis

(The General Practitioner and Internist)

The general practitioner is gone. But, unlike other dying breeds which became extinct because of over-specialization, the general practitioner is finished because he wasn't specialized enough. And good riddance. Though he has his myth safely ensconced in medical annals and people have fond memories of his gentle touch, he was less than a healing angel. Everyone concerned would have been better off had he, rather than his instruments, been sterilized, for he carried more disease than he cured, notwithstanding his boiling water routine at every house call.

Even in the good old days the patient must have looked askance at a healer who in all seriousness could prescribe such medieval concoctions as oil of eucalyptus or Syrup of Ipecac and other potions on the far side of nausea. To expect this physiologic insult to be tolerated by anyone less than a taster in a strychnine factory was asking too much.

These strange brews and potions plus the so-called gentle art of medicine were all the general practitioner had before he got pushed into science. But, as the saying goes, "Art is long and life is short." The art may have been a little exaggerated but no truer words about life could be leveled at the old G.P. During the plagues and epidemics, life was so short, doctors were selling (and lighting) more candles than cures. As far as the art goes, even today, it's not totally discarded.

37

When science and all else fails, this art may sometimes be called by another name at fifty dollars per half hour.

One of those artful dodges, the bedside manner, was a convenient fallback position. It gave the puzzled practitioner time to think up explanations (they explained in those days) for a horde of symptoms about which the doctor hadn't the vaguest. Often the "manner" was all there was to offer, unless it was extreme unction. But that too has passed since doctors rarely see a patient in bed these days unless it's in the intensive care unit. Then it's usually too late for science, much less art.

Eyeball Science

The old "doc," as he was affectionately called, was scientific in his fashion. He knew more by taking a pulse, listening to the heart, and watching the patient jerking around with St. Vitus dance than the modern cardiologist knows from putting a catheter into a heart. He would take a urine specimen only for the patient's sake, and on leaving, toss it out of the car window into the first ditch. He could tell better with the naked eye whether it showed a kidney stone, jaundice, or diabetes, and besides his car didn't smell like a urinal at the Salvation Army at the end of the day.

His most important scientific instruments were the stethescope and the thermometer. As to the stethescope, which more or less identified the doctor as a doctor, it was mostly for effect. Not five doctors in a hundred could pick up the sounds of pneumonia or rheumatic fever, unless it was so far gone the death rattle drowned them out. But patients were duly impressed—and believed in those two pieces of rubber tubing stuck in the ears as much as today's patients believe in the electrocardiogram. The present generation of doctors brought up on the din of the Stones, tone-deaf from electric guitar trauma, might as well put those earpieces in their nostrils for all they hear.

The other piece of scientific equipment was the thermometer, which, with proper snapping of the wrist, was a more impressive shakedown than the fee. The G.P. would never let the mother see the mercury, but would instead intone the numbers 104.6 or 102.8 in precise scientific fashion as if he were a NASA flight engineer broadcasting the countdown.

With or without science and notwithstanding the G.P.'s scientific instinct for diagnosis, the new specialists persisted in putting him out to pasture. They said he gave the whole profession a bad name. But underneath it all it only prevented one doctor from treating everything from measles to frigidity, thus sharing the wealth and making the world safe for dermatology, surgery, and gynecology.

The Count of 9

But the G.P. didn't go out with a whimper, not with six hundred million visits in the offing. He showed the powers that be that even when he did his damnedest, old mother nature still came through with more than he could put away. He pointed out that China, with hardly any doctors at all, is thriving to a robust 800 million, with only Mao's sayings, a little acupuncture and powdered rhinoceros horn. However, his fate was sealed; and the old squeeze play was on.

He was forced to give up home deliveries and left kitchen-table surgery to the specialist. This was his first big mistake—though the patient's salvation. With a foot in the door, the specialists speedily grabbed one organ after the other, symptom by syndrome. One day the G.P. woke up and found all he had left was taking the pulse, prescribing complicated concoctions, and surreptitiously lancing a boil or two in his back room. He did have a few bones thrown to him now and then. During prohibition he was allowed to hustle prescriptions of government booze for medical purposes only. It was said he rang up more sales than the whole Capone gang put together. (In 1932, with repeal, Roosevelt took even that away, and practitioners haven't felt the same about the Democrats since.)

It must be admitted he hadn't kept up with the times. After a few embarrassing incidents, where even the patients he had left dropped hints about not parking his beat-up Chevy in front of the house or asked about laboratory tests they'd just read up on in the *Reader's Digest*, he began to take stock. It hit him when the young snots he delivered insisted on a dermatologist for their acne while their mothers went to gynecologists for their lunar problems.

Thinking it was only a matter of image, since he knew that his younger colleagues—for all their degrees —were still doing the same snake oil and placebo routine, he made his move.

The Greening of the G.P.

First off, like any other endangered species, he adapted to survive. He changed the name of his game to the "family physician," organized into the American Academy of Family Physicians, and had yearly conventions like the specialists, getting sun poisoning and hung over at the same time. They discussed refresher courses and board examinations (that they were sure they could pass); displayed a red- and blue-ribboned sheepskin the size of a picture window; and even demanded equal fees. He also hired a part-time practical nurse.

But he still made house calls, didn't take the phone off the hook at night, took patients without waiting, and stayed up all night with the sick ones. Nothing happened and he was still being tipped in small change like a waiter.

He then took the big plunge. He moved to the medical arts building (downtown or in the suburbs), got a full-time nurse, wouldn't answer the phone himself, and got an answering service for night calls (which gave him the messages—but never on Sunday). For the first time, he noticed a few of his old hypochondriacs drifting back with new respect. The word had spread.

If It Walks in, Treat It

It was still not enough to pay the nut. Rent was going out of sight, carpets wore out, and the nurse demanded her cut. It was only then that it came to: "Damn the doctor-patient relationship, full speed ahead." The new family physician then went whole hog; widened his lapels, refused to make house calls altogether, got a new Mercedes Benz, and bought (on time) enough X ray, EKG, and other machinery to be on a par with the Mayo brothers. But most of all he began diagnosing and treating, whether it was needed or not. He was on the scene again—big. Not only that but since the family physician now specializes in the non-special his Academy is demanding specialist fees from Medicare and Medicaid.

As he found out it was big business—or no business. He wasn't exactly a wolf in sheep's clothing—but the kindly old mutton had learned a lesson. Now a trifle longer in the fang, less chummy, he was no longer Mr. Good Guy with the stethoscope and tongue depressor. If the public wanted speed, efficiency, and machinery, he'd give them more speed, more efficiency, and more machinery than they ever dreamed of. He still might not hit the diagnosis on the nose first crack out of the box and might on occasion miss it altogether, but he showed an in and out record that even a nose and throat specialist couldn't compete with. Instead of leisurely sitting behind his desk to talk and kibitz he was up and at them sashaying in and out of cubicles, ordering, advising, prescribing, and dictating into a portable tape recorder. His nurse weighed, measured, tested, and coded on a punchcard. They were out in a jiffy with the bill on its way to Blue Cross or Medicare. All he needed was green stamps and the A&P had better look to its laurels.

The change didn't come easily to this kindly, medical anachronism. He found it simple enough to press the right buttons for X rays, squiggly heart graphs, and blood-sugar readings, but there was one problem. Once done, the graphs, charts, and numbers were Greek to him—even with the short courses from the manufacturer. His ingenuity wasn't taxed for long. For a dollar or two a report (with a discount for ten or more) he soon arranged a little piecework deal with the best specialists in the business. They interpreted it all out for him and threw in a custom-made diagnosis to boot—like a Bowery clothing store sewing in Cardin labels. It was only tough on Saturdays and Sundays when the patient had to wait a while to learn whether he had a coronary or a bowel obstruction.

Cash as Cash Can

One of the great advantages of general practice even today is cash. It's not like it used to be since the insurance thing, but even Medicare patients have to pay for some part of their visit. And don't think those ten spots don't add up. Though some of the newfangled machinery may have the general doctors stumped, he's still a master at twirling the dials of the old office safe with confidence and agility. Most of those down-to-earth neighborhood physicians are honest, patriotic, and even charitable, but some do have a quirk when it comes to sharing the wealth with the Internal Revenue Service.

The G.P. has rarely been outwitted by the IRS in the hide and seek cash game. Shying away from computer billing was no oversight. It may be a time saver in the office but it tends to show evidence of an embarrassing nature in the tax court. The biggest problem for the family doc is where to stash the cash after the old safe is full. Some ingenious methods have been unearthed from which the keeper of vaults at the First National Bank could well take a lesson. Neither his office nurse nor his wife know where and how it is done. In cases of sudden death, it is gone forever, only to be dug up years later by some kids playing in the rubble of a torn-down neighborhood. On the demise of one neighborhood doctor another one bought what he thought was the biggest diathermy machine ever. He found it emitted no healing rays but was stuffed with a payload of ones, fives, and tens—which he in turn stashed.

In recent years there has been a logical demand for more primary doctors, as they call them. The reason is simple. Patients are going right to the specialists without the middle man and it doesn't work. For instance, a dermatologist faced with a simple case of chicken pox that didn't respond to calamine lotion until diagnosed by the third grade teacher is an embarrassment. Imagine the consternation if a patient with a bloody cough walked in off the streets into a gynecologist's office, or one with heart failure into the plastic surgeon's waiting room. These specialists get panicky when their kid's temperature goes over 100 or their wife has her monthly siege. The general man has his place, even with his sketchy knowledge of practically everything and his sure knowledge of practically nothing. He at least has the ability to keep in the back of his mind a lot of little signs and symptoms by which he could point the patient in the right direction.

Even so he ain't what he used to be. In this day of big business, the family doctor is now incorporated, in groups, with chairmen of the boards and pension plans. Also, as a full-fledged medical scientist now taking at least nine years of schooling and training, this dedicated man had to undergo a kind of metamorphosis. For his patients now need hardly be touched by human hands. So the dexterity to press buttons, adjust gadgets, insert tubes and needles, which takes the exacting expertise of a keypunch operator, became important.

Sample Him First

For the family doctor there are usually three steps to the final dissolution of a patient's ills. The first is the utilization of every conceivable piece of equipment that can be crowded into an examining room. Berman's Rule of Thumb Number 1 states that the speed of a diagnosis varies directly with the time spent being visualized, bled, and connected to electronic instruments. This first step takes a minimum of two to three visits. During that time if the patient doesn't respond to antibiotics, antihistamines, Valium, or all three, plus the electric jolt of the bill to date—it is obvious that he's really sick. Then comes step number two.

Step Two, Refer Him

This step puts the physician on his mettle. He must assemble all of these results into some order and make up his mind which category of the 57 varieties of surgeons, internists, or psychiatrists he must try his luck with. This takes yet another talent and skill—the fine sensitivity of a rat running a maze. Only after an equivalent number of rat years on the job can he expertly slot the patient somewhere in the area of a particular specialist. He must come close else his reputation suffers—especially when he's not too warm, like sending a scalp cyst to a brain surgeon. A batting average of 50 percent is acceptable.

Step Three, Send in the Forms

The keen diagnostic acumen of the top-notch family physician comes into play mainly at the third step. As an integral arm of the insurance industry—Medicare, Medicaid; government or private; compensation, social security; major medical or retirement—he must sit down in the quiet of his study and figure out which policy covers what. Here is where experience pays off. A minute slip could be costly to the future well-being of a physician and patient alike. If there is still a remnant left of the old doctor-patient relationship, it's here where there must be mutual faith and cooperation —us against them.

Super Geep

So the geep is dead—long live the family physician. But in the metamorphosis of the G.P. pupa, there was always one of the more ambitious type who wouldn't settle for the caterpillar status of the family doctor. It was butterfly or nothing for him. This G.P. had always been ashamed of his menial status in the medical household and knew in his bones that he deserved better. He had higher aspirations than capacities but was the one who took the quantum leap, skipping the family doctor bit and going straight for the leisure and status of the internist. If he had a few more years on the wards and a research paper or two under his belt, he'd be full-time professional material. But he wanted to have his cake and eat it too. He wanted to be a professor with his one or two patients a week to mull over in the privacy of his library and yet still be well tailored, Mercedesed, and Caribbeaned in season. So with a few years or so of residency (his wife working his way through) he memorized the necessary trivia he would never use, passed his internal medicine boards, and at last gained the "by appointment only" status.

The internist is usually fastidious and a dawdler par excellence. It's not that he can't make a decision, but he must do better than the G.P. In his two-hour history-taking sessions set aside for one visit (discharging the patient alone takes two visits) there are detailed footnotes to footnotes. He'll make use of every piece of machinery in his well equipped office, taking a dozen visits to make sure that the pain in the chest wasn't really caused by size E breasts stuffed into a size A cup.

If in Doubt Dawdle

There are some diseases labeled idiopathic (meaning no known cause), which the G.P. can only treat in a shotgun fashion, but which the internist pinpoints with a double barrel accuracy. This may sound like a make-work specialty, but if the G.P. can't even remember the geography of the organ and the super-superspecialist hasn't arrived on the scene yet, somebody must fill the void.

Headache, for instance, is a real symptom. It reflects maladies of a hundred kinds, from out-of-date eyeglasses to frigidity. It is not only of vague but of varying origins, as with women about to bed down with a raunchy husband or returning from a shopping trip with an over-used charge-a-plate. Yet one must not necessarily open every skull for this. An internist can spend years with a case like this even though temporary cures by a common little white pill of even more vague workings are not unusual.

Maybe a Dime's Worth

The patients that the internists usually get are hand-me-downs—when the practitioner is too busy or gets tired of seeing the same face in his office week after week. They have generally been gone over with the usual exhaustive lab and X ray work but not thoroughly enough to stop the internist from doing it all over again. He may hit 10 percent more diagnoses than did the old family physician and give an old patient a good five to ten minutes more but, in all candor, other than the extra sheepskin, there's probably not a dime's worth of difference, except in their fees.

There is one other very useful function the internist is good for in these times. He can get a patient in the hospital where the family doctor can't. Family doctors have been eased out because they have diploma-poor blood. The practitioner with only one diploma is a hospital untouchable—if he's seen around too much, it gives the institution a bad name and puts its accreditation in jeopardy. So if the family physician has a really sick patient, it's to the internist for a hospital bed. It's better than having him expire in the office. But there's some compensation; though they can't admit or prescribe, the F.P. can see and talk and even charge the patient. It's sort of a double check that works to everyone's advantage but the insurance company's.

So that curious G.P. excrescence on the body medical is almost all gone. And though in a sense one may say good riddance, the sad excuse for what has replaced it, the F.P., is little better—nor is his professional life expectancy long-range. As a mere adjunct of the pharmaceutical houses, insurance companies, and government (big and small), with his duties limited as an information and directional service for the specialists, and his instruments, computers, and machinery gradually taking over, he too may soon be obsolete. Everything they can do the computer does better. And already on the drawing boards is the AFPB, the Automatic Family Physician Booth (Orwell forgot this one), which will be in every shopping center by 1985. Coin operated, it will weigh, photograph, X-ray, bleed, aspirate, peek, and poke, and in ten minutes come up with the probable diagnosis on a punch card, the insurance forms enclosed, which specialist to go to, with addresses and an appointment slip. It'll also make change and give a receipt. The only thing it can't do is solemnly look a patient in the eye and murmur, "Hm-m-m-m."

6

The Adventures of Mac the Knife:
The Barbers of Scal-pel
(Surgery and Anesthesia)

There is an old proverb in football: When in doubt, punt. There's an older one in surgery: When in doubt, operate. From the look of it, either the surgeon has become the greatest Doubting Thomas of all times or we're sicker than we think. Undoubtedly it's better to have cut and lost than never to have cut at all, which not only keeps the surgeon technically trim, but financially fat. The one word that makes it right with his conscience and the world is "exploratory" and from the statistics one would conclude that surgeons are more pioneering than Lewis and Clark.

Somewhere along the evolutionary trail the sabertooth tiger must have had a hand in the shaping of the surgeon's personality. Bits and pieces of the big cat still prowl in the mind and motives of those devotees of the scalpel. There is the slow twitching of the striped tail in the surgeon's stalking of his hemorrhoidal prey. There are the sounds of predacious claws ripping at the soft underbelly of a checkbook or insurance form. And last but not least, the slitlike pupil in the tawny eye is as concealing as a surgeon's flat gaze when he tells you what he's about to do, what he's already done, or what went wrong.

We all know that any patient who comes in with any complaint to any doctor is fair game. And cutting at will is part of the long and lucrative tradition of the surgeon. Should five years of training lie fallow be-

49

cause of some ethical taboos? Should his deft skills with a blade become rusty, so that when there is a real need for surgery the patient might suffer a heavy hand? Every fair-minded patient knows surgery is a calculated risk—frequently for the good of the patient. But let's not entirely forget the good of the surgeon.

Lively Knivery

Understanding little of the surgeon's personality, both colleagues and public condemn him as knife-happy. However, if one comes right down to it, isn't the psychiatrist couch-happy or the family doctor lab-happy or X ray happy? It's like saying that an electro-cardiograph bought at considerable expense is not there to be used on a Medicaid patient, even if he comes in for itching piles. Sure, some surgeons are knife-happy and the more lively the knivery the happier they are. But should he be indicted for malpractice because of a mere pittance of a mortality on a long-time favorite, the appendectomy? Isn't gambling the spice of life?

This is not to suggest that the surgeon is all gambler or that he is not the most responsible of physicians. Surgeons are drawn to their specialty by specific psychological quirks, not the least of which is shown by a stainless steel glint in his eye and a certain incisiveness in his touch.

He is not the queasy sort. His predecessor, the early barber surgeon, was the one who enjoyed handling leeches without panic as blood poured from every orifice. In those days he blanched not a shade as he hacked the leg off a victim with only a pint of anesthetic brandy to help. He'd plunge the white hot poker into a festering maggot-filled bullet wound as if he were spearing a boar. With the advent of chloroform and ether there was a more refined approach, but the surgeon's basic nature hasn't changed.

We are not speaking of the Fancy Dans who remove wrinkles and shape noses, nor that anal compulsive, the proctologist, fixated on the one puckered orifice. We are speaking of that swashbuckler, the general surgeon, who ranges over the entire corpus from ingrown toenails to removing ten feet of troublesome bowel.

Hacking Hazards

In surgery, as in most of medicine, intelligence is no great drawback, nor logic a prerequisite. It's actually by some sort of dead reckoning that the diagnosis is made. From then on, it's cut it out and get it over with. There is no interminable dawdling with pills, capsules, and injections. But as fast and decisive as it sounds, it's no free ride. If he tends to have tics and a hair trigger temper, there is ample reason. The wear and tear of the daily orgy of clamps, catgut, and blood leaves an indelible mark on his vulnerable psyche.

The surgeon also has the misfortune of double exposure. His every little mistake in the operating room is there for all the world to hear about via the assistants' bad-mouthing or the nurses' gossiping. The monthly Mortality and Morbidity Conference doesn't help; the word seems to spread as though on prime time by a national network. Then, as a final insult, there is the fishy eye of the pathologist looking over his shoulder, asking embarrassing questions of the most incriminating nature as to why it was removed, what was left in, and how come the victim didn't make it. This unenviable position demands a thick skin and a hard skull as well as the surgeon's reputed steel nerves.

On the other hand, the surgeon's less benighted colleagues, the G.P.'s and cardiologists, go scot-free.

They can palpate, percuss, bleed, wire up, and digitate every orifice, then push their pills and potions in the privacy of their office with no one looking and broadcasting. And neither they nor the bereaved of the less fortunate of their patients ever know the reason why.

The psychiatrists, internists, and other self-styled intellectuals of the breed *Medicus americanus* put the surgeon down as merely a technician, a professional bloob (as the surgeon in turn puts down the urologist or proctologist). But he cares less for the opinion of those eggheads when he is so highly respected by bankers, brokers, and Mark IV Continental salesmen alike. In fact, he feels more comfortable with them than with his patients or his colleagues. Those business entrepreneurs are men of substance and understand not only his flamboyant style but also the definition of a reasonble fee—all the traffic can bear.

Thumbs Up—All Ten of Them

So he isn't a genius, but neither does he rank as low as the gynecologists or the urologists. If surgery doesn't take that much brains, it at least takes dexterous hands—hopefully as good as a seamstress's; but good hands are as hard, if not harder, to come by as good brains. It's no secret in the clan that a good one half of all general surgeons who practice on live patients have still to overcome their morning shoelace-tying problems—whether that first string goes over or under the second.

It is not impossible for a youthful aspirant to a surgical career to go through an entire five-year residency with less surgical ability than Jack the Ripper. But a little bribery helps in climbing the surgical residency if the grandfather gave a building to the hospital or an intern married the hospital director's niece. Somehow or other these golden hands get along—and luckily old mother nature covers for the sins of the cutter, especially if there's a better-than-average intern or two pitching in at the operating table. Otherwise those facile fingers would be running a mortality neck and neck with kamikaze pilots.

The chief, the house staff, and even the nurses know each and every one of these surgical misfits and it's always a big joke in the operating room (if not to the unconscious patient) when a second-year resident must occasionally take over in midstream. Luckily, some clumsies have a nagging conscience or are just too scared to go beyond the bread-and-butter hernias and skin cysts that a pea picker could learn to do in two weeks. (Albert Schweitzer trained an assistant fresh from the jungle to do most operations as skillfully as he himself.)

The real dangerous surgeons, however, are those who have trouble handling a salad fork but who are gutsy enough to tackle open-heart surgery. The AMA has yet to come up with a legal or moral means to restrain their ardor much less their mayhem—until and unless they retire. Retirement could solve the problems if there weren't more where they came from. But who retires? And who will tell a seventy-year-old surgeon with rheumy eyes and a tremor with a 9 on the Richter scale (the San Francisco Earthquake was only 8.5) that he can't do a gallbladder or a thyroid with thousands of them under his belt?

No matter the age or skill of a surgeon, sometimes both his courage and his conscience must rise above the fatal if human little errors at his work table. They're not really his fault. He has family problems like everyone else and though he may have had one too many the night before, he must muddle through once again. The results of the drinking surgeon are not as bad as those of the sober fumbler but may inspire less confidence, as the patient about to go under the knife looks up into those bloodshot eyes.

As Mal as the Worst of Them

But under the best conditions, surgery is no longer the care-free cutting of yesteryear. For though the prime target in the malpractice game is the gynecologist, orthopedist, neurosurgeon, or anesthetist, the general surgeon is right up there with the worst of them. The astute negligence lawyer gets a wider variety of worthy cases from the general surgeon because our hero plays with more varied vital organs. The ham bone is connected to the thigh bone and when too much thyroid gland is removed with those other little parathyroids stuck on the back side, the whole system can go berserk. The resulting combination of spasms and cretinism is enough for a people's advocate to retire on for the rest of his days.

Surgical cases may not yield the malpractice volume of their better rated competitors—but the awards are just as juicy. For this fact of surgical life the incising healer may pay a yearly premium sometimes approaching the price of his Miami condominium (in New York it may go to $40,000). In the meanwhile, his internist or cardiologist colleagues who can do as much harm with a few cortisone pills and again go scot-free. But the strangest fact of all is that the suits come not from the tough, emergency surgery, or from surgery done in a not-too-sterile office by the young and inexperienced, but actually from the easy elective operations, done in the best university hospitals by board-licensed or -qualified experts. Even the family doc who does all the cutting he can in the smalltown hospital or in the privacy of his city office rarely catches it like the surgeon. It's gotten so that even good surgeons duck the tough cases. Any physician in his right mind who responds to "Is there a doctor in the house?" should have his insurance rescinded, if not his license revoked. And no more Mr. Good Guy at traffic accidents.

The surgeon himself admits that he is not the thinker, the Oslerian medical philosopher type. In fact if he followed in the footsteps of some of the old masters he'd be hard to handle without net and shackles. One of the patron saints of modern surgery was, of all things, a junky. Professor William Halstead of the "Big Four" at Johns Hopkins was as peculiar, if fastidious, in his dress as he was in his surgery. He had his shirts sent over weekly to be laundered in Paris just as every capillary in his surgical incisions had to be neatly tied with the finest silk. It was always a question whether this hop head's punctilious mind drove him to cocaine or if it was those sniffing highs that made him see every ooze as a gushing artery, thus laying down surgical principles which are still universally used.

In any event, the institution which celebrates him explains away its professorial addict as being in the finest tradition of self-experimentation. And maybe it was. What difference if his "high a day kept the jitters away." If surgeons in these high mortality days had any sensitivity at all they'd all be mainlining after each operation. This habit was not (or is not) unique with Halstead; and if anything can give one the cold shivers it's the fact that medicine has a higher percentage of junkies than any other profession on earth.

To Cut or Not to Cut Is Hardly the Question

The guilt-edged personality of the surgeon is drawn to quick results. Some of his more righteous colleagues smile knowingly and snidely attribute the rapidity of his cures to the paucity of the disease. The implication of this, of course, is unnecessary surgery, which he hotly denies. Nader claims there are over 3.2 million unnecessary surgical operations a year, costing five billion dollars with about 16,000 deaths. The surgeon on the other hand argues that it can't be proved. Even so, if less than one-third of all operations are unnecessary, the figures are tolerable. Anyway, even those that are unnecessary, such as tonsillectomies (1.5 million a year) and appendectomies (.5 million a year) are performed on organs which are at best expendable but at worst possessed of the potential to get the patient into trouble.

The statistics on whether a procedure is necessary or not, or is a success or not, may be tough for the layman to come by, not to mention the investigative reporter or the law. But the merciful attitude of the surgeon is, "Why dig into all of this and worry the ailing with statistics which will only depress (or excite) him?"

Recently another potential headache has been making the rounds to the effect that surgery creates more surgery. This may be true but it's added more and more to the difficulty of convincing a patient to go under the knife. If it gets any harder it might even necessitate anesthesia in the home just to get him to the hospital.

Ether-eal Healers

Unlike yesterday, the surgeon is today dependent on a well paid and silent partner. We're not talking about "ghost surgery," which is yet another subject, but how many patients know who puts them to sleep? Other than those few seconds before he injects the Pentothal and clamps a mask over the patient's nose, there is little contact between anesthetists and conscious patient—until the computerized bill arrives.

The anesthetist is an outwardly stable (if inwardly jittery) and rather pleasant fellow. His predecessor in medieval times was not the intellectual type but the one who gave the shot of brandy and a bullet to bite on, using his muscle to restrain the agonized patient as the knife was plunged in. The current version seems to smile perpetually, whether from good-naturedness or the effects of too much "laughing gas." Yet since he seems always to be holding his breath, not knowing for sure if he turned the right knob—will it affect the liver, could it explode today, is the patient getting enough oxygen, will there be brain damage, why the arrythmia, will there be cardiac arrest? His main concern is—which complication will the surgeon blame on him. To this day anesthetists know as little about what that depressant gas or fluid does to the brain stem as they do about its effect on the other vital organs. They have every reason to be constantly aquiver, for it's been proved that most anesthetic deaths are due to their error. With thirty to forty thousand deaths a year to their credit, and a malpractice premium up with the best of them, they can't get enough young M.D.'s to replenish their waning numbers.

But there has been progress. The fancy equipment and new gases are paying off handsomely. In the days of chloroform the big question was whether the incision was to be made in the OR or in the morgue. The sleep is not quite that permanent anymore, but since it's nip and tuck on the tough ones, the fees are proportionate to the risk the patient takes: The greater the chance of his not coming out of it, the higher the fee.

The one-half billion dollar business called anesthesia has two ongoing occupational hazards besides the temporary ones like being sued by the government for price fixing. The first is written all over his pallorous face, as he's probably inhaled enough noxious gases in his lifetime to float the Goodyear balloon (though whatever it does to his psyche it seems to have no effect on his libido—he's known as the raunchiest operating room chaser on those long nightly vigils between calls). The second hazard is libel by proxy, as the surgeon takes his name in vain as the cause of everything postoperative—from gas pains, nausea, and vomiting to shock, wound disruption, and postoperative psychosis. But he takes it like the technician he is, for the hiring surgeon is his bread and butter.

Quicker Than the Eye

In the old days, a surgeon was known by the smallness of the incision and the speed with which he made it. Frequently, the endearing soubriquet (mainly by women) was "Buttonhole Goldstein" or "Seven Minute Monte." It helped build many a practice. But as the fourteen-minute gallbladder record began to tumble, the boys got a little sloppy and tools, sponges, and other operative paraphernalia began to disappear, only to crop up in the patient's wound or abdomen. This of course doesn't build reputations—except with reporters and judges—and was one of the original malpractice claims. It's still high on the list, but not like before. For now the newer nickname is "Manhole Charlie" with incisions as far as the eye can see, taking as much time and anesthesia as the patient can bear. Pieces of rubber glove or, as in one instance, the lens from the surgeon's eyeglasses are rarely left in anymore, unless the pressure of some business or romantic engagement has the surgeon more preoccupied than usual.

The Fed and the Feeders

The guts of the surgical game are feeder G.P.s—those who refer patients. For the first twenty years of practice, the surgeon spends much of his life building a stable of feeders dedicated to the proposition that, results be damned, there is only one surgeon under God. The care and feeding of these practitioners is an art not taught in any surgical residency and as closely guarded a secret as a CIA assassination plot. It's also the sign of the successful surgeon. If he can wine, dine, charm, ingratiate, solicit, golf, travel, and strike the right deal with a group of these pillars of the profession, he's in the money. Since the surgeon's prestige depends on the amount of time he spends in the OR it soars with the size of his stable. If he can maintain their loyalty against the discount offers and the attractions of other surgeons, especially the younger, better trained, and even more capable ones, the operating part of his life is just a happy interlude. The only time a surgeon would swap his wife is for a faithful feeder, who is much harder to come by and still harder to keep.

Mal-fee-sance

It is a base canard that surgeons invented fee-splitting and that they corrupted the simple-minded practitioner. Historically, it has been shown that fee-splitting is not original with the American surgeon; it's an ancient and dishonorable tradition. It was known back in the Han dynasty in China even before acupuncture, when the herb doctor used to demand a little something (called "squeeze") when he sent a tough case to the moxa specialist. And it's been with the profession ever since. Although it is generally condemned by the AMA, they did provide a nice little loophole. In their bylaws they say that if a general practitioner helps the surgeon (they don't say how) they can send a combined bill, so either way the family physician will get his. Of course, the general practitioner in Middle America does a great deal of surgery himself, so he charges for both and gets it coming and going.

For that special young man with ambition and a yen for the high life, and the flair of a sadistic nature, surgery is the thing. It not only yields a marvelous gross and a beautiful bottom line but the deep satisfaction of a fine pickpocket in using the dexterity and sensitivity of those busy fingers, taxing the brain very little. The more academic types know that there are many more research grants available to surgeons than to any other three specialties combined. And for the superstars of the profession, whose images warrant front-page stories and pictures in the doctor's favored newspaper and *The Wall Street Journal,* the rewards are not only pleasing to the wife but does wonders for the ego. There's also an excellent opportunity to broaden one's horizons through travel, as the surgical association's peripatetic seminars go to the farthest corners of the earth totally tax-deductible.

All in all, it is a rich career for those with the mind of a banker, the fingers of a blackjack dealer and the ethics and guts of—well—a surgeon.

7

Pubic Health:
Wombats of the Western World
(Gynecology/Obstetrics)

A gynecologist's intellect, it's claimed by his colleagues, stops at the pelvic edge. Once he has learned to recognize that pear-shaped structure in the pelvis, flanked by those two egg-producing troublemakers, he's almost in business. Then he has only to memorize his hormone tables, which are only slightly harder than the multiplication tables, and he's home free. Putting these two together, his whole stock in trade is to remove what he recognizes and prescribe what he memorizes. This takes about as much brain power and skill as an apprentice kosher "chicken flicker" who flunked his national boards. Ask a gynecologist about the anatomy, physiology, or pathology of any organ above the belt or below the pubis and his stare will be as vacant as if you were questioning a flagpole sitter on the fourth law of thermodynamics.

The gynecologist picked the best of all possible worlds when he delved into the pelvis and decided that that old symbol of fertility was his to have and to hold —and to discard when necessary. Unlike the more complicated specialties, here is a neat little package, highly expendable and almost inert (except in heat or in pregnancy). It is so easily accessible it could be plucked out blindfolded with fewer complications than an office visit to a dermatologist. Once spayed, other than a few stubborn hot flashes and drenching sweats, "there rarely is heard a disparaging word." Whatever other few benign complications may come along (like frigidity, phlebitis, or gangrenous hemorrhoids) can always be blamed on her delicate hormonal balance, her pregnancies, or her husband. The latter is the popular culprit.

The gynecologist is a special kind of specialist, with his healing capacities residing in neither his golden hands nor his agile mind. The difference between success and failure with *female troubles* depends more on a Barrymore profile, the sculptured coif of a Liberace, or those big baby blues of a Paul Newman. This is an Rx that practically any female disease, including the most intractable pruritis or that new diagnostic fad, vaginal shingles, responds to better than antibiotics or strawberry douches.

The Ace of Spays

But the Adonises of the pelvis know well that there are occupational hazards to this show biz specialty. Invariably their popularity waxes and wanes not according to results but according to the times. In the '20s the women flocked to the slick-haired Latin, Valentino type. In the '40s the long, lean, Gary Cooper, Jimmy Stewart gynecologists were the ace of spays. And now in the '70s it's that insouciant devil-may-care Redford sting, which has the garden club members panting for some simple pubic anomaly—any excuse just to be examined by one of these centerfold types. It's still a sad day when the aging specialist wakes up and finds that he is last year's model; then it's a shrunken practice, attracting only old patients with everything already out. He must then fall back on that operation of last resort, the vaginal face-lift, with neither the glamour nor the fee of the plastic surgeon.

Though nothing will stop the ailing (or well) woman from beating a path to the male gynecologist's door, the militant feminists are working him over as they have Pope Paul (for his anti-birth-control *Humanae Vitae*) and Teddy Kennedy (for Chappaquiddick). But there was trouble even before that Madame Ovary of liberation, Gloria Steinem, came on the scene. Her less than genteel gender now belabors and berates her less liberated sisters with a constant harangue that a *she* should not be caught dead in a *he's* office. If she does, she deserves every flash and flush of the empty pelvic syndrome and, as they warn at the consciousness raising sessions, *caveat emp-ty*. The macho feminists maintain that the male gynecologist, for whatever kinky reason, has some sort of clitoral envy and is driven to orgiastic delight notching his curette handles with every ovary excised. Even so, when the chips are down they'll go "a long way baby" before they'll let a female operate on them.

Mirror, Mirror on the Floor

But, the rank and file of the most militant Germaine Greer breed of feminists who do patronize their own female womb-bat for their six-month overhaul don't even trust *her* completely. They have come out with a handy, do-it-yourself, instruction manual for self-examination ($2.95 at your local consciousness-raising headquarters)—with mirrors yet. To get a simple Pap smear is a contortionist nightmare that the Russian Olympic gymnast Olga Korbut couldn't manage. Picturing some of the flabby militant feminists in this rather awkward upside down maneuver is a scene only the old burlesque comedians could do justice to.

In recent years, science has made the lady doctors' lives much less risky. For instance, during their diaphragm period (sometimes called their blue period), they fitted those devices with well disguised fear and trepidation. The gynecologist always waited for those inevitable days when an irate husband would storm in with the news that a little unwanted stranger was on the way. It was not an infrequent happening, for diaphragms were not only an indignity to the passionate female but as chancy a fit as a mail-order suit from Hong Kong. Those domed rubber cups either floated around as if designed for a midget virgin or couldn't be stuffed in with a shoe horn, with or without the usual accessory lubricants of creams, foams, and jellies.

So the pill, the brainchild of the male scientific community, is now the perfect solution. There are allegedly a few minor drawbacks such as cancer or phlebitis, but there is absolutely no physical risk for the male.

Another great relief for this specialist's overloaded brain is that the once formidable derring-do of an abdominal hysterectomy (minor surgery to a real surgeon) has now been almost foolproofed. Without scars the womb is simply everted through the vagina, pulled through, snipped off, and *voilà!* Few gas pains, no adhesions, and everything is perfect—well, almost perfect. On occasion a little vaginal foreshortening occurs whereby the husband may have some difficulty gaining entrance unless the maneuver is digital—or he is midgetal.

However, there are a few lumps in the gynecologic gravy, not the least of which is dealing with an hysterical tigress climbing the monthly wall with her raging hormones (the Greeks didn't label that fertility fount *hysteros* for nothing). And, of course, at the other end of the line is the bedraggled, flushed, and flashed ash of her former self the menopausee, frequently amenable only to a carload of hormones or a lobotomy.

Fees for Cervix

When it comes to the organ snatch, the militant feminists may have a point. Next to tonsils the uterus comes first in the "out" department. But though almost half of all women over forty are advised to get rid of it, some few resist. Along with the 700,000 surplus uteri, about half a million will have the works—tubes, ovaries, and all—deleted in one fell swoop at the bargain price of 3.95—million that is. But thanks to the skill of the gyno, only twelve hundred will follow their deleted organs to wherever the good organ heaven is.

Gynecologists were among the first to be accused of organ rustling. Naturally they soft-pedal this all the way to the ethics and grievance committees. They can prove that what they remove, suspend, tighten up, or lay fallow, is in strict accordance with the fashion of the times, can always be supported by some improbable technicality, and is clearly this side of malpractice. They blame the whole base accusation on those holier-than-thou, full-time university professors in the warmth of their ivory wombs. They counteraccuse the Ivory Uterites with being out to get the working stiffs, who just can't make it cutting out only sick stuff. In any event, an unnecessary hysterectomy is a tough charge to make stick. It can never be proved whether a uterus as healthy-looking as a masseuse in a Finnish sauna has not bled or hurt from the invisible curse— the hormone. When up against the ethical wall, the gynecologist can hide behind that "ole debbil" estrogen that makes *hysterikos* (suffering in the womb), as the Greeks put it, "rage like an eagle rather than coo like a dove."

But even without the womb snatch legalizing abortions is the best thing that has happened to gynecology since pregnancy. It's put a new show on the road without changing the cast. The same characters as before are still doing the abortions but it did make it easier on their nerves. Now out of the locked-office, kitchen-table operation and in the legitimate glare of the operating room, there is no hot breath of the vice squad or the IRS blowing down their necks. Not only that, but as luck or popular science will have it, it can be done now with a foolproof suction-cup procedure that a student nurse could administer. This combination gives the womb-bat the same license to steal as he had in his illegal abortion days in a third of a billion dollars annual take.

That Course Called Inter

But abortions haven't been the only recent windfall for the enterprising gynecologist. They didn't let the Masters and Johnson sex wagon go by without a look-see. These forward looking gynecologists were not going to miss a bet, combining business with pleasure.

Since there is no licensing of these practitioners, not only is every two-bit family physician giving it a go, but every non-professional hustler who can memorize the working parts of the Arch of Venus is getting into the act. It has now grown so fast and so large it's difficult to tell a sex center from a massage parlor. As M and J warn, "less than one in seven hundred of these therapeutic houses are legitimate." Most of the non-gynecologic professionals snicker at it (if they aren't doing it) and the psychs (who are already working the sex side of the street) consider the whole deal, M and J included, a school for scandal.

But it's right down the gynecologist's alley. It's easy, lucrative, and—whether they admit it or not—fun besides. The only preparation is reading M and J's *Human Sexual Inadequacy* and having the waiting room magazine rack filled with *Penthouse, Playgirl,* and a smattering of hard porn such as that eminent physician "Cash and Comfort's *"Joy of Sex, More Joy,* and probably a *Still More* coming in the future. The clinics may even be arranged for off-hours—so as to give their most objective teachings on the touch, smell, and taste of sex—upside down and backward, with or without a flying trapeze. What's more, the price is right. At the most famous sex clinic, M and J's St. Louis Reproductive Biology Research Foundation, there is a five- and six-week waiting period with no money-back guarantee for the course called Inter at a bargain price of $2,500.

Most of these clinics swing high, wide, and handsome. There are nude encounter groups with professional models and demonstration sessions with patient models. In the more resistant cases there is a last chance treatment with a well trained surrogate f - - ker who comes with impeccable credentials and letters of recommendation.

One could go on and on with the professional life and style of the gynecologist but there is also the obstetrical side to him he'd best like to forget. Though gynecology was once just the tail end of delivering babies, that tail now wags the dog. When the complications caused by doctor obstetrics became as numerous as the babies delivered, pregnancy was on its way out as a lost art. But since no one else would do the dirty work, the combined hustle of the OB-Gyn specialty came into being. Both, of course, originally came from the midwife, but it didn't take long for the non-obstetrical end to shuck the unglamorous low-income, midnight, midwifery for the more prestigious, lucrative, scheduled midknifery. Any gynecologist with half a brain (and there are many) who still does OB, does so just to pick up a little Gucci money on the side, and though it's not big, it's steady.

The Mother Nudgers

The job of obstetrics doesn't demand much. With or without his presence the child comes through—some say women were better off dropping *it* in the fields. And though considered less a physician and more of an accomplice to a natural act he is still allowed all the rights and privileges of his M.D. He can subscribe to the AMA journal and even get in on convention vacations with a tax write-off. As one of the many low men on the medical totem said:

> His is not to reason why,
> His is but to pull and pry.

By choice, the obstetrician leads a life somewhat between an all-night disc jockey and a charwoman. By a whim of nature or maybe as a just punishment for aiding and abetting human continuity, deliveries are mostly in the dead of night, with many false starts from frightened first-timers keeping the poor man on the road as much as in the delivery suite. The night-after-night routine of waiting for an unformed fetal Godot to make up its mind could not be tolerated by a human of less than bovine temperament. (In the national health insurance scheme in London, obstetricians are inducing labor after just so many hours and before weekends and holidays.)

Then there is the final insult, at the moment of truth, being deluged by a gush of amniotic fluid, mucus, and afterbirth that a Roto-Rooter man wouldn't put up with. Besides this nightly hairshirt existence, the extra-onerous pleasure still falls to the obstetrician to be the bearer of glad tidings to the newly delivered that she is the proud possessor of beautiful bouncing twins—the Siamese kind.

A Melon Through the Eye of a Needle

As if this weren't enough, these poor souls have another monkey on their back: the young marrieds, products of the sixties, who once sowed their oats of grass, now demand natural childbirth. These wilted flower children, yoked to each other but removed from the parental payroll, obviously didn't learn a thing from any of their former naturals, food or love. The female of the species, now in her late twenties, still in her faded blues, insists she must feel every millimeter of stretch as that lemon-sized orifice dilates to let a watermelon-sized thing push its way out. She says she likes it and maybe she does; who can account for the tastes of pregnant women who are known to doll up their martinis with cherry-topped whipped cream? Not only does the poor obstetrician have to take this leftover hang-up with a straight face but that once free jock that got her into it must sweat it out with her.

She learns the Lamaze breathing technique as she once learned her Hare Krishna. When the time comes and the camel-sized baby's head is threaded through the eye of her vagina sans anesthesia, she is screaming like a banshee. He meanwhile is in a catatonic trance afraid to open his eyes. This sharing of a nightmare, so they say, engenders future serenity, love, and the ultimate in pure parent-child relationship.

One thing for sure, he'll never forget this experience, especially if he must go through the bloody ritual of a Caesarian section. Male members of that togetherness team must rank high among those four million post-natal alcoholics and they certainly lead the pack of those hundred thousand or so husbands who abandon ship each year. One sure thing, she'll think twice before another one of those drugless trips is taken.

Survival of the Foetus

Pity the poor OB man. After all those years leading a life worse than ignominious and being looked down upon by colleagues and nurses' aides alike, his future is now dimmer than a hooker's hallway. What's left after unisex, homosexualism (married yet), zero population, and now the cruelest blow of all, the pill. Obstetrics wards are being rented to the Salvation Army and delivery rooms converted into abortion clinics. The iced pram cometh.

There just couldn't be more. But don't underestimate these hard-luck Jonahs. The *coup de grâce* malpractice comes to the delivery man. These creatures timid by nature are now scared to death of every mother of every idiot child who yells birth injury. In Maryland, one of the great states for malpractice, an obstetrician is being sued for four million dollars by a baby without all its marbles he delivered with his own hands some eighteen years before. Obviously, obstetricians are now so gun-shy they won't apply the forceps until the recalcitrant little devil is about to suffocate—which may mean more malpractice headaches.

The OB Complaint

There is less and less reward in the Job-like job of the obstetrician—but being underqualified and unsuited for other gainful employment he can't give up. With the withering away of his practice, the malpractice suits, and playing the waiting game, he's come up with ploys like the other boys. As to his creature comforts and life style he no longer lets that little stranger's tardiness ruin his rest or his night out. They'd better be born on their scheduled birthday or they're in for some scientific shenanigans that'll make their scalp stand on end. It's becoming common practice to reach into the womb, slip a monitor on the unborn's skull, and scan to see whether the little stranger is really in trouble or just dragging its feet.

On the subject of income, the obstetrician dug into

history. When in doubt, do unto others what was done unto Caesar which obstetricians maintain has little or nothing to do with the doubled fee of Caesarian sections (but in prepaid clinics the usual birth canal is the general route of escape). Whether needed or not, a Caesarian section isn't too bad a deal for the female —whose vanity goes from top to bottom. With less stretching and tearing—there's only a hairline scar to show for it all.

Gynecology and/or obstetrics would be an ideal specialty except for one thing—women. The office work is simple, deliveries and surgery a snap, diagnoses are made by the patients themselves and the hormones business is good in all seasons. But that one big rub sticks in there.

The wombat is faced with a lifetime of unpredictability that's absolutely predictable. Portnoy's mother was only one of many. Though indestructible she accounts for the bulk of the six hundred million doctor visits a year and she's healthier sick than a Russian shot putter. Portnoy's sister's monthly ills can make of her a sickly pathetic Camille—unless she's in love when she's about as frail as a dray horse in heat. This is not to mention Portnoy's mother-in-law complaining of flashes and sweats but who has a backbone like a musketeer. Otherwise, the life of the Wombat— is a pear-shaped ball.

8

From Fraud to Freud to Fraud:

A Boon for the Idbegotten

(Psychiatry)

It's been said that a psychiatrist is a Jewish doctor who couldn't stand the sight of blood. But this hardly holds up; the Jewish faith doesn't believe in the second coming while psychiatrists have all but announced the messianic nature of their calling. Unlike the ordinary physician who feels he is the right hand of god, the healer of the mind accepts no such secondary role.

From the beginning, psychiatry has been in the hands of the sorcerer and the exorcist—and from the looks of it, it still is. From witch burning to lobotomy it's reflected a theater of the absurd. Since its halcyon days, when kings and conquerors were in thrall to their shrinks, trial and error has been its means, with error coming out on top. Lately it's been a steady downhill course, lit by rare flashes of brilliance such as TA (transactional analysis) and fornication therapy.

Freud, the megalomaniac father of modern psychiatry, was also the first to switch a specialty from medicine back to a kind of priesthood. Hypnotism, his first gambit, was blatantly plagiarized from a vaudevillian hypnotist, Mesmer (who had made the reverse switch from the priesthood to medicine). Though he might not recognize what his latter-day disciples have done to his original idea, Freud would not be displeased with the marvelous shell game they made of it. Psychiatry had always showed great side-show possibilities. It was a cinch after the first break-through with the hysterical little girl supposedly seduced by her father. This was followed by Oedipus, dream analysis, id, and the rest of the gobbledpsyche. Even Barnum was contemplating replacing either the Gypsy Seer or the Mood Mad Monster with this new midway attraction until the AMA put its foot down.

But the latter-day generation of psychs knew that if they didn't tone down the sex-and-circus aspect, not only couldn't they count on referrals from their straight colleagues but even the average neurotic wouldn't buy it. The sound basis of psychiatry—mother, father, and masturbation—was left untouched but it was obvious that by itself it couldn't compete with Christian Science or Billy Graham. So in a businesslike way the psychs injected new gimmicks and ideas that the public would buy.

Give Us Your Bored, Your Kooks, Your Gullible

First they impressed on their colleagues that, when stumped for a diagnosis or just tired of a nasty patient, the couch was always ready. Then they hustled the lawyers and courts into accepting psychiatric excuses for murder, rape, and embezzlement. With these two innovations, business picked up and the hour had to be streamlined to fifty minutes to squeeze in another two sessions a day. Finally they went direct to the man in the street with offers he couldn't refuse. Jazzing it up with "touch sessions," Esalen, yoga, and even good healthy Fornicotherapy it really paid off handsomely. Psychs may have missed out on a few good things like Reich's Orgone box, but they won't repeat that mistake: They're now giving the Primal Scream, Transcendental Meditation, and just about anything else that jumps out of the box a real look-see.

So cerebral a calling as psychiatry was bound to attract some kinks, oddballs, and even a little human debris. But who would have thought they'd take the whole show over? Maybe it should have been expected since it was often medical students who couldn't memorize *Gray's Anatomy* and who were still bed-wetters who went into it. These are not absolute pre-requisites and a bartender's common sense may come in just as handy, but for the student it was killing two birds with one stone—learning a trade and getting their heads on straight at school rates. They did suc-ceed in learning the rudiments of staring straight ahead while dozing, without falling over, at fifty dollars per —which is something—but somehow they never man-aged to unscramble their ill-gotten brains.

What Are Little Psychs Made Of?

Psychs can't be judged by ordinary standards. Besides their own mental aberrations which drew them to this specialty, their day-in, day-out contact with the screwed-up and addled hasn't done much for their sense of values. They teeter on the brink, not exactly sure of right from wrong, much less normal from ab-normal.

Not long ago at one of the founts of the great art of mental "healing" in Chicago, a psych made head-lines that shocked his medical colleagues, though not his psychiatric ones. He was caught coming out of a supermarket with two frozen New York strip sirloins —one under each armpit. Because this wasn't the first time, the police had to book him for neglecting to pay the $6.95. He was not committed, as his patient might have been, for he claimed in all sincerity that he always defrosted his steaks so they'd be ready for the broiler by the time he made it home. He just forgot to check them out and there is nothing abnormal about that. He was, of course, let off without a fine.

This steak episode hardly raised an eyebrow among his colleagues. As the American Psychiatric Association asks, "What's normal?" And what is normal for a specialty which invented the strait jacket for those too active and the electric shock for those not active enough?

The Practice of Lily White

In some circles the psychs are maligned as peculiar, liberal, leftish, and offbeat, which, judging by the petitions they sign, may be true. The worst put-down of a psych, young or old, is the label conservative or Republican. They no longer sport winged collars but what's so offbeat about blue jeans at the office? His lifestyle is suburbia and his business ventures in stocks, nursing homes, and condominiums would make a banker look radical. Though his practice is 98.8 percent white and 80 percent college-bred, this in no way proves he isn't liberal; his door is open to anyone —who can pay the toll. (Either Chicanos, blacks, and hillbillies have some kind of built-in mental health, or misery is the psychiatric cure everyone's been looking for.)

There is also a popular misconception that all psychs are a little crazy. It's not hard to understand why they go into psychiatry when they can't stand touching the sick but their aversion to hospitals is the essence of sanity. As much as most doctors enjoy hospitals with their pleasant camaraderie, professional challenges, and especially the ten-dollars-a-minute pit stops, the psych does not. But he's crazy like a fox. He knows that mental hospitals are full of the disturbed, alcoholics, drug addicts, and criminals, who are not only sick but dangerous. Who needs it? The psych man-hours spent in alcoholic centers is about 0.2 percent of their time; with retardees 1 percent; drug addicts, 0.4 percent; and the elderly, 0.1 percent—how's that for crazy? They know that if people really want to get well they'll somehow manage to get to the office, and if they're too tough to handle, they belong somewhere in an institution.

From Sludge to Fudge

Much of the healing effect of a psych comes from his own personality. And since this effect is at best rather minimal, there's something wrong somewhere. Where else but in his training? Since his business deals neither with measles, muscles, nor microbes, how could dissecting everything from earth worms to cadavers, and massaging everything from hearts to prostates, help treat a paranoid? With just a little training in Jesuit logic and some psychology on the side, he'd have been better equipped to treat minds not much less sound than their own. Freud himself, who never wanted to practice medicine, thought analysts could better spend their early years in social work or genetics.

To help redress this basic error, the first few years of analysis are spent trying to clear out all that scientific medical school sludge, if only to replace it with the fudgier stuff of psychoanalysis. It's generally unsuccessful. Repeated searing of the brain with shock therapy could probably do it better, faster, and cheaper.

Lay as You Go

What conceivable advantage does a medical training have over a stevedore's apprenticeship in that popular new psychotherapeutic tool called Fornicotherapy —where the chandelier and the couch are used interchangeably. Here, training in a bawdyhouse could do him more good than in a clinic. The well known New York analyst Martin Shepherd in his book *The Love Treatment* says if the goal of the therapist is to help his patient grow and learn, any and all means are valid. Needless to say, not all psychiatrists have subscribed to this type of "grow and learn means" as a healing measure. Some killjoys such as Siegler and Osmond in their new book, *Models of Madness,* claim that "psychiatry has sunk below the bare minimum standard of behavior." But this is probably just intraprofessional jealousy.

This particular model of madness (which paradoxically has little to do with the Horney school of analysis) isn't as bad as it sounds, and it may be the best use the psychiatric couch has been put to. At least it adheres to Hippocrates' first law of medicine— if you can't help them, don't hurt them. The patient doesn't break out in a rash as with penicillin, or with deafness, as with streptomycin. And if, as Freud claims, sex is the cause of it all, why can't sex be the cure for it all?

Not to dwell on this kind of penile servitude, but since the prominent psychiatrist Dr. Hartogs was shamefully sued for $350,000 recently (by three ungrateful patients) his technique has evoked some minor communication problems that are now being debated within the profession. A new terminology has already sprung up which is so simple everyone understands it. For instance if a neurotic tells her mother she is "all f--ked up," it wouldn't mean what it regularly implies, but only that she had completed her treatment. If a business executive was told by his therapist to go f--k himself, it's not meant as a nasty expletive, only that he is ready for self-analysis.

With any new therapy questions are constantly raised. First and foremost, how many of those special fifty-minute-hour treatments (with only a ten-minute break) can a conscientious doctor give? Such devotion, even at the age of forty, not to consider older professors, is above and beyond the call of Aesculapius. And from the newspaper accounts of Dr. Hartogs' cases he obviously chose with more of a roving eye than a therapist's intuition. This poses another question. Could he be as effective with the anxieties and depressions of women who look like Fanny Brice as he could with those who look like Marilyn Monroe? If not, who treats those poor unfortunates with even less physical than emotional endowments?

The female psychiatrist practicing fornication treatment—if she were really good at it, and it does take talent—would be sure to have a waiting list longer than the Happy Hooker's. And talk about fees—Blue Shield would have to put in for another added premium. Ultimately, the question would be posed—would Blue Shield ever pay for this kind of prescription, especially in the very disturbed younger males with chronic psychic priapism who may require treatment seven days a week and twice on Sunday?

The Cash and Carry School

Though this therapy shows the psych as an ordinary erotic male, when it comes to cash on the barrelhead they're neither erotic nor erratic. Everyone pays, just like at the supermarket. Different schools may deviate from Freudian principle in one way or another, but when it comes to fees, they're all in it together. There are no discounts to friends, relatives, students, nor to colleagues, retardees, or other unfortunates.

Though no internist, surgeon, or cardiologist has ever been accused of over doing charitable work, they have never charged another doctor. But for the newer fornico-therapists it's "no pay—no lay"; and in the words of their immortal psych saint, "paying is part of the cure." And since one-third of all patients in analysis come from the medical profession itself all would-be analysts must pay for their *good-psyche-keeping* stamp of approval.

Yet with all of this built-in clientele, psychiatry is probably more financially disadvantaged than any other medical specialty. It doesn't have that old, whatever-the-traffic-can-bear, free-enterprise aura. To be locked into one room ten hours a day, averaging hardly more than $100,000 a year, isn't medicine as it should be practiced. They rightfully feel their talents exploited compared to their neurosurgical or urologic colleagues who can knock down a cool two to three thou for a routine two-hour skull or prostate opening.

But the psychs are not unresourceful. Having gone through that useless and confusing training in medical school they figure why not use it. What isn't the brain lord and master of? So if the anus itched and nothing helped—it was psychosomatic. Psychosomatic medicine took into its generous fold everything from the broken femur of the accident-prone to the hard-driving tycoon's ulcer. But there is a little hooker here—two can play at this game. As the psych begins to treat bodily ills, the family doc and the internist began playing the psych game and getting good at it. Most of their patients are as healthy as Mark Spitz anyway, so now they're prescribing more Librium than Anacin. It's still cheaper than the weekly psyche session.

The Group Grope

The psychs also lay their eggs in more than one basket. They've come up with a dandy called "group therapy." Here, ten or more patients are couched together at thirty dollars a head. This is more like it—a neat $300 an hour. He acts no differently than he does with a single patient, talks just as little, and officiates like the chairman of the board. He may have to break up the more violent arguments or cut off the longer harangues; the only drawback is that, unlike the one-to-one sessions where he sits at the back of the couch, he's too visible here to sneak a catnap. Some sessions also wind up in carnal, if not consciousness-raising orgies in which they all become "by love possessed." Here the psych's main job is keeping himself out of entangling alliances and disengaging the writhing bodies in time to tidy things up for the next session.

There have been complaints that this method causes much fetish exchange among the group with some patients catching more problems than they lose. But it's no skin off the psych's nose. Some patients are going to feel better and some worse whichever way they're treated. The important thing is that these new ploys bring his earnings up to a level at least respected in the profession.

The Patient Is Not for Curing—Psych 22

After a patient invests five or ten years and from $50,000 to $100,000, there is always a nagging doubt in his (and the family's) mind whether it's just the money or the problems they're relieved of. In surgery the patient knows he's OK when the stitches come out; in pediatrics, when the rash disappears; in orthopedics, when the cast comes off. There's no such point in psychiatry. As the months extend into years, the patient has enough time to talk himself out, and explain his uniqueness, which is what selfish neurotics are all about anyway. But even that can't go on forever, and some patients and families don't take the couch lying down. The battered-psych syndrome with stab wounds and broken bones by patients has become a new social phenomenon. In one Boston clinic assault on psychs has risen 30 percent.

To the psych, cures are irrelevant, which is of no embarrassment and a neat little source of continuing sustenance. As they put it—theirs is not the run-of-the-mill healing art and time is not of the essence. The intricacies of the mind are not as simple as broken bones or burst appendices. Whether ten sessions or ten years, it seems more like a psych 22: If they need a psychiatrist and know it, they have enough insight to do without it; but if they have that insight and don't try to get cured, they're sicker than they think; and if there is no such thing as a real psychiatric cure anyway, they may be able to take care of these problems themselves but they feel worse and will probably never get any better.

The simple word *cure* causes the psych a slight frothing at the mouth. Among themselves it's a *sotto voce* topic. The best of them can never count their chickens—till the last hymn is sung. That same Dr. Hartogs of the "new school" thought he had a real success with one of his more outstanding patients, Lee Harvey Oswald, until that backsliding episode in Dallas. Richard Nixon was Dr. Hutschnecker's showpiece—a cure that made it to the White House—until he began to show cracks that widened and split right into his medulla oblongata. When he wound up with that "sainted mother" valedictory, *Air Force One* should have flown him direct to St. Elizabeth's rather than to San Clemente.

Cure is a sometime thing even with full-fledged cum laude graduates from the Menninger or Mayo hatch. Their alumni are known to revert back too often to sill-clinging, bridge-jumping, or arsoning. Some of those adolescent sexual problems treated at the Phipps Clinic who "just had a little fling with their mother's

underwear" may wind up as transsexuals wanting
nothing more for Christmas than two front teats.

A doctor works till the setting sun,
But the good shrink's work is never done.

But if the psych has not the satisfaction of the
cure, neither does he have the agony of malpractice.
A judge or jury can see where an eye is missing or a
leg is deformed but could they judge it the psych's
fault if a child-molester upgrades his tendencies to
adolescents? Should a jury award a paranoid anything, if after treatment he degenerated from imperson-
ating Albert Schweitzer to doing Charles Manson? Even
if the psych hurts more than he helps, who can pin
it on him? (In a recent study, 29 of 32 suicides were
prescribed for by doctors just weeks before.)

Paranoia by a Landslide

As far out as they supposedly are, the psychs even
took democracy to an unheard-of extreme. Though it
was the psychs who made the mugger, the arsonist, and
the patricidal child acceptable as sick, they have gone
themselves one better and, for the first time in medical
annals, they *voted out* a disease. They didn't cure, ex-
punge, or obliterate it—they voted it out. On the convention floor of the prestigious American Psychiatric
Association's annual melee, by a show of hands, they
declared homosexuals off the critical list of mental dis-
orders and made them into Sexual Orientation Disturb-
ances (whatever that is). It's like the AMA convention
declaring 862 to 78 that malaria no longer can give
you chills and fever.

All of these shenanigans have made patients and
families leary not only of the psych, but of the whole

medical profession. OK, so there are no sure cures, but then again, they can't seem to come up with causes (etiology) either. They've got dozens of theories, schools of thought, and institutions based on everything from trauma *in utero* (*or exutero*) to Ma and Pa guilt, to the Primal Scream and Gestalt, but will the real crippled id ever stand up? If there are no sure causes and no sure cures, what kind of a science is this?

A Billion Dollar Business and a Ten-cent Cure

Did Freud really pull a fast one? Were Jung and Adler dupes? Is Nathan Kline from Rockland State Hospital trying to do in a billion dollar business with his chemicals? If not, how can a lousy ten-cent tranquilizer lay all those beautiful, dream-world theories and hypotheses to rest? What about those inferiority and mother complexes, fantasies, birth traumas, dream analyses, and Rorschach tests that told you everything you always wanted to know about your hang-ups but were afraid to ask?

It's come to a pretty pass—and an embarrassing one. Here is the only specialty in medicine built on intellect rather than microbes and tumors, and they're secretly gulping more mood-changing pills than their patients. The psychs aren't starving yet, but because of a few simple concoctions like Librium or Valium, the whole gig may be up. Those colorful little "dolls" taken three times a day and at bedtime are freeing the neurotics from the couch quicker than pot freed the kiddies. It's opened the cages of a thousand loony bins, letting half of their inmates trade their strait jackets for wide lapels. Except for their more rational behavior, one couldn't tell them now from a successful analyst. The tranquilizer has done more damage to psychiatric practice than that other pill did to obstetrics.

But what's more, how can a psych explain it to five million neurotics who worshipped the fifty-minute/fifty-dollar hour like a true believer? What excuse do they make when a Lourdes-like pill lets a "crippled id" throw its psychiatric crutch on the pile? But the real ignominy of it all is that twenty-five-thousand highly cerebral psychiatrists lie exposed by a simple pharmacologist who probably couldn't even pronounce transactional analysis. It's a disaster. Chemistry may soon be all the way in and analysis all the way out. Even medical schools are looking for professors who can handle a test tube rather than a Super Id.

Sick Transit Psych

With all of this, the psychs aren't yet jumping out of windows (more than usual) and it'll be a sixty-minute hour before they give in to a little Thorazine or lithium. They're not even jumping to conclusions on the flimsy evidence that a few million neurotics feel better on the pill than on the couch. You just can't count out a group which has survived so long on so little. Don't underestimate a specialty whose checkered history begat Mesmer, whose hypnosis begat Freud, whose analysis begat Jung, whose dementias begat Adler, whose complexes begat Horney, whose self-analysis begat Esalen, TA, hallucinogens, Primal Scream, and the Philippino psychic surgeons.

As the pill makes its steady inroads, the psychs shift, parry, and dodge like a punch-drunk welterweight. They'll try anything and everything until the last patient is tranquilized. They've already started a whispering campaign that the pill causes a depressed libido in the male and hottened libido in the female (which it does)—how's that for a marital happiness pill? They also spread the rumor that the men who made the crucial decisions for some of our most successful corporations were on tranquilizers. As things get tighter, the psychs are making more noises in the direction of psychosurgery. The brain is their beat and if behavior is to be changed they'll do it, even if they can't stand the sight of a razor nick.

In their panic they've gone way off. They're accepting all sorts of children, not only the usually disturbed late adolescent, but those riven by the demons of puberty. Psychs were never the most stable doctors but who would think masochistic? The pediatricians unloaded all their childhood problems and ran like a purse snatcher. Pediatric societies will most assuredly vote psychs their humanitarian award of the year—maybe of the century.

These are the times that try psych's roles. But with their ingenuity, they'll surely come up with a different hoax for different folks. If they don't, the lay psychs will, without the benefit of medical schools or state boards and at reduced rates. And as long as voodoo, Christian Science, acu, or what have you is still in demand, so will the psychs be. He may not be very fruitful but it seems he will continue to multiply.

9

Open Hearts:

Send Flowers

(The Heart Doctors)

Like the old-maid school marm and the high noon, two gun outlaw, the cardiologist and heart surgeon are the oddest of odd couples. Who would expect the very proper practitioner of the gentle art of listening for a decibel's difference between a heart's *lub* and *dub* would mate with the wildest and woolliest surgeon of them all—the knife-slinging carouser who'll sit up all night waiting word that his heart snatcher has a live one for carry-out? For a quivering bowl of jelly like the cardiologist to be hooked up with a Cooley must be as hard on his coronaries as if he caught his daughter with Alice Cooper.

The cardiologist was originally spun off from the most conservative of internists. Even the funereal quietude of the internist's life was a bit too hectic for his jittery personality. How could one concentrate on more than one organ at a time, and still decide which one was sick? It was just too confusing to have to decide whether a hiccup was from a liver abscess or last night's hot pizza.

A giveaway to the personality of the cardiologist is the number of Hen Medics attracted to the specialty. Naturally this type of genteel art where only one organ need be listened to and tapped out, with no probing of microbe-infested orifices, suits the female temperament to a tea. A *she* with her special, indecision-making intuition is even better than the most waffling *he* at contemplating the squiggles on a mile-long roll of EKG paper. But it was this most unlikely old-maid temperament that started the whole cardiac surgical circus—a bit like Helen Hayes starring in *O Calcutta!*

Dr. Helen Taussig of Johns Hopkins, though a pediatrician and a pussycat and now one of the grand old dames of cardiology, happened on it all by fiddling with X rays, EKGs and specimens of hopeless blue babies for twenty-five years. Even the most prim and fussy male heart specialist was glad to get those off his hands and into hers. As a typical spinster doctor puttering around trying to be useful, she was tolerated by the cardiologists as long as she kept away from the paying adult stuff.

Dr. T., No Abzug She

No aggressive Bella Abzug type, Dr. Taussig went unheeded by her male superiors for ten years before her ladylike insistence mothered the father of heart surgery, Professor Alfred Blalock. Thus began the strangest marriage of convenience since Jackie Kennedy and Ari O. Blalock would still be dabbling in the thymus gland, a long forgotten dead end, if Helen hadn't catapulted him into worldwide glory by showing him how to make pink babies out of blue. It's said she had to write the procedure down each step of the way so that he could memorize it even with a hangover and follow it in the operating room.

This great man opened up the whole new field of heart surgery. A Southern gentleman to the core, he also graciously protected the gentle Helen from the unladylike hurly-burly of worldwide attention, taking the brunt of it on his own broad shoulders. After the first few babies had turned from blue to rosy red, the professor ran like a thief in the night, setting the style for all heart surgeons of the future, scooping up all the kudos, honorary degrees, cash prizes, medals, and headlines before Helen was even satisfied that the operation was really doing the trick.

But gentleman of the heart that he was, after a few years of being wined and dined (he was more a winer than a diner) by medical (and real) royalty, elected chairman of this and editor of that, his place in history secured, and the real story beginning to leak, he thought it high time for her debut. With a head and conscience as clear as the morning after, he let Helen out of the bag with his usual show of southern gallantry. Though now silver-thatched and emeritus—grounded—she is at last getting her faint praise as Mother of Surgery of the Heart. And as a regular on the honorary degree circuit, from Sweet Briar all the way to Bennington, she is also a household word in the *Ladies' Home Journal*—if not in the *Annals of Surgery*.

To Jog or Not to Jog

Up until Harvard's Sam Levine and Paul Dudley White (the cycling octogenarian who treated President Eisenhower's ailing heart), most cardiologists wouldn't let a coronary go to the bathroom much less jog. If those bed indentured cardiac patients, in oxygen tents for a month, had been made to swim the English Channel (both ways), their mortality couldn't have been worse. After fifty years of this "advanced" therapy by the best brains in the cardiac business, those two proper Bostonians got a few out of bed and—lo and behold—most of them recovered faster and lived better. Then with old Paul Dudley leading the way, they began jogging and biking with even better results. The race between ambulation and rigor mortis had been won.

If malpractice had been in vogue then this specialty would have had a quicker death than they led their patients to. The mousy fears of the heart doctor had made more heart cripples than skiing makes leg cripples. Today a seventy-year-old patient plays two sets of tennis three months after his bypass operation and will live better (if not longer) than a thirty-five-year-old coronary fifteen years ago. This still isn't great, but it's better to have jogged and lost than never to have jogged at all.

Scalpel Loose and Fancy Free

It took a shell-backed entrepreneur like Denton Cooley (known as the fastest knife in the chest) to really put all the mousy fears about that "delicate" organ to rest. As he holds that mythological seat of soul, love, and life in his hands, he knows well that it's tougher than a mother-in-law's will. After all, what muscle can beat continuously for seventy to ninety years without a rest, responding valiantly to the ups and downs of cigarettes, coffee, and sexual acrobatics, plus the strains and ravages of married life? Anyone who has ever watched the maneuvers of the more clumsy heart surgeons (and there are a few), knows that this organ can take a beating a Sumo wrestler couldn't stand.

As the cardiologist oozed out from the internist cocoon, the Barnums of the surgical suite came thundering out by way of the ordinary surgical swashbuckler. But with their panache, even general surgery was too strait-laced to hold them. After Blalock's show-biz start in the early '40s, Charles Bailey, the Hanneman cardiac whiz from Philadelphia, became famous for sticking his finger into a rheumatic heart (he was a burned-out star at forty). The specialty then took off for fair.

Now the Barnards and Cooleys play it like a passel of Saudi sheiks. For them a $100,000 heart transplant is a mere bagatelle. And why not? After cruising around the world with princesses, Broadway stars and moguls, one gets bored with lesser figures. After getting used to the front page, seen escorting Barbara Walters or Gina Lollobrigida to the April in Paris Ball —they can't go home again.

When DeBakey operated on the Duke of Windsor, Cooley's P.R. man trumped his ace with a rash of medals, the last from the now fashionable King Hussein. As would be suspected, Barnard's decorations reach from his neck to his navel. Given the pace they've set, they may not last much longer than Bailey. While they do, they may be faulted for their flair, their style, or their lust for power—but never for their nerve— both in and out of the OR.

B.C. (before Cooley), the old-fashioned general surgeon had to take two belts of Jack Daniels to get up his nerve to ask for a postmortem. No such problems for the brethren from Houston, Palo Alto, and Capetown. These steely-eyed charmers who blithely ask a parent for an eighteen-year-old motorcyclist's heart while it's still beating would seem to have as little shame as the hospitals that charge five hundred dollars for treating a DOA (dead on arrival). Then they do an operation on a barely alive patient, when the best he can get out of it is a 30 percent chance of living one year, if he gets off the table alive.

The Fibrillating Ferdinands

At one time the cardiologist hid his patients from the surgeons like a mother her draft-dodger son, discounting the press accounts of the miracles of heart surgery all the way.

But the disabled heart patients couldn't resist the lure of living it up again, if not more so, as the heart surgeon glibly guarantees. They take the gamble. Then the cardiologist either loses a patient or goes along— so he goes along. Once the case is snared the heart surgeon as is his nature bypasses the cardiologist and the cardiologist doesn't much care. This is one specialist who returns the patient, unless it's a king, queen, or a senator. For the ordinary patient, when the operation is over, the surgeon may never be seen again but he receives and accepts all the credit, and as far as the cardiologist is concerned, he can have it.

Unless the family insists on his presence (which it usually does), the cardiologist sees fit to go to Asia Minor or be incommunicado the day of the operation. On those blood-and-guts mornings he arises with a shaking palsy and an angina of the entire body. Furtively he puts on a thick layer of his wife's Estee Lauder Rosy Blush before he ventures forth so his state of semishock is not obvious to the operating room team. Just seeing the surgeon handling the object of his affection has a trying effect on his own heart. Alternating between triphammer pounding and stopping dead altogether, he is as much concerned about himself as the patient.

On those mornings of truth for which the Barnards chomp at the bit, but which the cardiologist dreads, he finds himself longing for his quiet rounds in the coronary care unit, the oxygen tents quietly humming, everything placid and even the patients a nice neutral gray. How did he, a man of peace, ever get into this shouting, scurrying, flaming-red haze of an OR focused on a hysterical surgeon who's handling a heart like a football? In the sixth or eighth hours of this *danse macabre,* the patient may have to be brought back to life two or three times—and the cardiologist at least once.

Flashing back to his salad days, what a pleasure it was spending a quiet morning in a shaded office, devoting his entire time to one nice old senior citizen (with a failing heart) too weak to even complain. Occasionally a little excitement: Checking a pacemaker to make sure it's not another of the many thousand defective ones or even regulating the dosage of digitalis. Unlike his counterpart the surgeon, he may not be attracted to hunting big game in Kenya or gambling at Monaco, but his quiet pleasures of bird watching, sailboating, and cookouts are not without kicks.

The Headline's Where the Heart Is

But alas, open-heart surgery has now permeated every nook and cranny of America, and the cardiologist is part of it. Every two-bit hospital that gets a case wants to try it. Some have, with interesting if not living results, and at a cost even Blue Cross can't afford. But that doesn't stop either a yahoo surgeon looking to make his name in Dubuque or a hospital administrator looking for prestige in Oshkosh.

Of course the tight-sphinctered Harvards, blue-nosed Yales, and the tawdry aristocracy of Johns Hopkins or the Mayos are well into heart surgery. But no panhandle whoop-de-doo for them. No stooping to such public displays as transplantation, even if they had the talent. Only the *nouveaux* like Stanford's Shumway or the Houston "oilers" would do something that gauche. Those "better" institutions may finger the heart, put plastics in, catheterize it, and even stoop to bypass it (after five years of trial), but never, never will they transplant it. It wouldn't have worked anyway. A Back Bay-er or Baltimore Brahmin would never accept donors from anyone but a Boston Cabot or a Carroll of Maryland and it's rumored they're not easy to come by.

Only in Texas

Today the new surgical mecca of the heart is none other than that moneyed metropolis—Houston, Texas. What other city could fit the role? Cardiac surgery was built for Houston and Houston built for the cardios. Where else should the skill, money, publicity, and the grand way of life meld together in one whirlygig.

Though Barnard in Capetown beat the Houston brawlers to the punch, it wasn't long before the Texans overcame. But Houston surgery is a world unto itself, and the ongoing feud as to who was the fairest of them all (in Houston) had to be settled first. According to the headlines, Cooley tried to grab the artificial (mechanical) heart idea as another first to show who was numero uno, and Dr. Michael DeBakey countered with the cry of "foul," claiming it was euchred from a researcher at the NIH where he has his clout. Though doctors in glass houses rarely throw stones, this impasse went all the way to the Supreme Court where the handsome young Texas-born Cooley won hands-down over his foreign (Louisiana) rival. In keeping with their style Big Mike didn't sit around and sulk. At sixty-eight he upped to Europe and married a beautiful actress less than half his age.

In any event, heart transplants or mechanical hearts (now Barnard ups the ante putting in an extra heart) was only to gain a little attention in the fraternity, whet the cardiac's appetite, and keep the patients flowing—south. Though Barnard and Shumway still persist in their deadly game—not the Texans. With that old

LBJ shrewdness, as soon as the transplant come-on had shot its wad, it was discarded like last year's Neiman-Marcus sable.

There's No Business Like Bypasses

This year's password is *bypass*. In cardiac surgery, no matter who starts what, it's who cashes in that counts. Once grabbing the spotlight, all else flows. What is flowing even better and more than Houston oil is bypass millions, and the way it looks, there's billions where that came from. The new answer to one of the biggest killers in medical history may yet become the biggest killing in medical economics. Though the "bypass" for coronary heart disease is similar to the one discarded twenty years ago, it's now back by popular demand and doing a land-office business. It has not been conclusively proved yet, but then neither has aspirin—and billions of dollars worth of that little moneymaker has already been sold. If tens of thousands of patients believe and are waiting—who among those altruistic, reticent, selfless cardiac surgeons is going to disillusion them?

On the world scene a balance of power is being struck. Barnard now holds Western Europe, the Arab states, and white Africa, and Cooley has the United States, Latin America (non-Communist), and black Africa. Lately, Cooley has been making inroads into the new rich Arab states with his recent bemedaling by King Hussein in Jordan. But neither worries about the other. They're birds of a feather dominating the surgical summit and are living it up as no other physician ever did. And they will probably go as they went— in high style.

Go—Go Gone

Heart surgeons are show biz till they're lowered away. Their passing will out-Louey Louis Armstrong's last journey to the promised land. One can see it now; laid out at the "21"; bedecked with hearts of flowers; Leonard Bernstein and the Philharmonic in a fortissimo Mahler's First (The Titans). Gathered around the bar are the beautiful people with misty-eyed, tiaraed royalty up front fortifying themselves with Lafite Rothschild and dolloping beluga caviar waiting for the liveried gray Silver Ghost Rolls procession to begin—with not a wet-eyed cardiologist in sight.

10

From Hags to Bitches:
A Nose By Any Other Name
(Plastic Surgeons)

At one time, though primped and rouged by the embalmer, man went to his grave looking somewhat like the image he had lived with all his life. Today God wouldn't recognize what He hath wrought. If He had wanted each and everyone one of us to look like Sophia Loren or Paul Newman, who was there to stop Him? Variety has always been the spice of His life and if He made nine thousand different species of beetles, it was only natural He didn't want three billion look-alike humans. But lo and behold—here come the wrinkled, the lop-eared, the flat-chested, and the potato-nosed trooping back to the heavens unwrinkled, bosomy, button-nosed things of beauty that even St. Peter couldn't identify.

And now lately imagine the shock of having sent down a nicely bepenised and scrotumed Johnny only to have it come back a vaginad Janie. On the other hand it would be a sight for sore eyes to welcome Phyllis Diller back even with just minor corrections.

The Hand That Shapes the Nose
Could rule the World

Though medicine has more immediate crises to worry about—like malpractice and National Health

Insurance—thwarting nature as the plastic surgeons do poses some moral problems, especially for a profession that does the illegal or immoral only when absolutely necessary.

The National Science Foundation is scared to death of genetic engineering and its effect on society. But don't they realize how faces and figures change psyches as surely and much quicker than chromosomes? Do they have any idea what the impact of plastic surgery could have had on history? Would Hitler have been such a madman had that puttylike face been converted into the visage of a Robert Redford? Where would England be today if the bulldog countenance of Churchill had been changed into the romantic profile of John Barrymore—could he have kept the women at bay, much less Germany? The whole feminist movement might never have been if Betty Friedan had looked like The Bardot. As the AMA and their National Science counterparts are debating the potential problem of genetically producing a brave new world, let them never underestimate the power of a nose job.

As with most of medicine, morality and ethics goeth before the buck. Like fornication therapy and vitamin B_{12} shots, there are no national, international, or even sexual holds barred in cosmetic surgery. Plastic surgeons have not and will not let a good thing like cosmetic surgery pass them by. Medicine has done beautifully so far by catering to the patient's fears and pain but what a windfall it'll be cashing in on their vanity.

Strangely enough, cosmetic surgery was not just another gimmick the profession promoted, like the annual checkup, but a legitimate, spontaneous surging up from the grassroots. Not that those Fancy Dan surgeons wouldn't have abandoned their humane burn-and-accident surgery if they had caught on to their vanity fare sooner, but the public beat them to the punch.

Vanity Fair

Thinking back, it was right before their eyes and they didn't grab it. Patients spend over a billion dollars a year on cosmetics to make an impossibility presentable and it washes off overnight. Why not something more permanent or at least renewable every five years or so—without scars yet? What middle-aged house frau wouldn't want to wake up every morning and with a dash of cold water on the face look as fresh, slim, and clear-eyed as Liv Ullmann? Who needs to go through that masochistic routine of the morning mirror and the struggle to cover up, smooth out, and paint over; then dismantle it every night only to see it return with the dawn's early light? Besides the aesthetics of plastic surgery, it's like money in the bank. Considering the savings in lotions, fresheners, shadows, shrinkers, softeners, uplifts, two-way stretches, and the like, it's a bargain.

They say it started very simply. Once again it began with the Jews. This myth was naturally given credibility because of Christ, Marx, Freud, and even Jack Benny. And as usual with one of those many miracles of scientific serendipity (looking for one thing and finding another) it occurred in the strangest place. In the case of cosmetic surgery, it's said an ordinary nose and throat man stumbled on the nasal bob by accident and modern cosmetic surgery was born. It happened that he was operating on a now unknown Jewish princess for a deviated septum (to this day deviated septa are the standard excuse) but there was a hump in the way. Not thinking it mattered, he shaved off an eighth of an inch of nasal cartilage just to get on with the job and in six months she was engaged to a doctor. (It could have been called a nasal engagement.)

From there the rich and the not-so-beautiful took over. If they could buy a decorator to redo their

Sardinian beach house why not use a little of that wherewithal to redo themselves and and not spoil the scenery. Why should they have to drape (or dodge) every mirror in sight. Now it's gone even beyond this. It's an equal rights thing even done in military hospitals.

A Nasal Foreign Policy

Being a thing of beauty and a *goy* forever is not only a princessly aspiration, but seemingly the goal of all ethnics. Cosmetic surgery now crosses national boundaries and takes precedence over national prestige, Arab refugees, or oil blackmail. War or no war, plastic surgery now passes through the demilitarized zone in Syria and Egypt and goes from the west to the east banks of the Jordan. Kissinger could have speeded up the whole process, had he just led by example. He may have added a laurel cluster to his Nobel prize. A couple of plastic surgeons from Israel, sent to Saudi Arabia or Iran, would not only have changed the face of Arabia, but no doubt led to a permanent settlement of the economic and military problems of the Middle East. After baccarat, U.S. banks, and Las Vegas hookers, those oil-rich Arabian knights are sure to go for the ethnic nasal cure.

Though it was a nose and throat man who first came across the nasal gold mine, it was the plastic surgeon who saw cosmetic surgery as the miracle whose time had come. With little adieu, he just took it over —nose, breast, and face—and has been adding to it ever since.

As useful as plastic surgery was in the past, cosmetic surgery is its future. Other than those few who still practice useful plastic surgery, even the older ones are into the beautiful people and have all but forgotten how to treat cleft palates or do reconstructions.

A Stitch in Time

Surgeons may be made but cosmetic surgeons must be born. Only the chosen with the talents of Karsh or Stieglitz and with the mathematical precision of an Einstein could have put together the faces (if not the brains) of some of their glamorous patients. Only a millimeter separates a smile from a leer. To the movie or TV camera, a single stitch makes the difference between the wide-eyed warmth of Gina Lollobrigida and the gimlet eyes of Mannix.

Those so gifted in plastics show their tendencies early. As most kids of yore wanted to be firemen and policemen and now stockbrokers or doctors, the parents of plastic surgeons say it's always been a tossup whether their offspring would go into decorating or into their chosen field. The best, or at least the most popular of them, are living examples of their art. The Tom Reeses of the profession, tall, even-featured, blondined and wrinkleless even as they age, epitomize the model face saver. It would be discouraging for a potential beauty to have to confront a bejowled, wrinkled, potato-nosed surgeon and go to the OR wondering why he didn't do a little for himself. Even in their dress, they are the fanciest of Dans and make the ordinary surgeon (no slouch) look like he came off the rack at Korvette's.

There's nothing ordinary about these miracle workers. Stars like the Brazilian super plasto Ivo Pitanguy work hard, but only a few months a year. They play hard the rest but only at St. Moritz, Longchamps, and Antibes; but work or play, it's only with other jetters. It's always been a wonder how they withstood the four years of the mundane, the dull, the routine of medical schools.

Nasal Transference

You can't avoid comparing the plastic surgeon to the psychiatrist. First, he cures more neurotics and purveys more happiness by shaving a sliver off the nasal cartilage than six years in analysis (which shaves a lifetime off the pocketbook). Second, in both there is no professional courtesy except with each other. (The plastos do at least keep each other bagless and wrinkle free. In certain select cases, say if another Phyllis Diller came in to be redone, the publicity in *Women's Wear Daily* would be worth a little discount.) Then if the case goes awry (and it does happen, say, with one silicone breast pointing south and the other north) they have a problem on their hands that might need the combined talents of Menninger and Nathan Kline. Most plastos have a good grounding in psychology and a working knowledge of psychiatry. Of course, there are also differences between the psychic sicks and the plastic slicks. The surgeon always knows his results and takes the good with the bad; the psych's failures don't show, they jump. The psych never knows if he helped or hurt; the plasto sadly enough may know after the first dressing comes off.

You Can't Tell an Ethnic
Without a Scorecard

Today, plastic surgery seems to have gotten out of hand; it now poses worldwide national dilemmas. For some reason, there's hardly an ethnic group that seems happy with what it was born with. If the prosperity lasts in Japan, there won't be a slant-eyed beauty left either in the geisha pleasure house or the Kyoto ranch house. The robust Italian mamas and Argentinian señoritas are having their baby-stretched abdomens teenaged, their breasts maidened, their heavy-hammed rumps Bardoted, and their cellulite piano legs Dietriched. Their pasta-fattened tycoon husbands have their bowels short-circuited so they can eat a bucketful of pasta fazool three times a day and stay slim as a noodle.

There is also no doubt that old age has gone out of style. Many of the aging stars (like Tallulah Bankhead, who looked thirty for over twenty years) go to their plastic surgeons for nips and tucks as frequently as they are checked by their gynecologists.

The Lift Is Mightier Than . . .

It was a living cinch that show business celebrities and the Blaze Starrs would beat a path to the star chambers of the East 70s or the chic waiting rooms of the west coast Belair emporia conveniently close to Chasen's, Romanoff's, and the Beverly Hills Hotel. Since Ole Blue Eyes had his transplants, MGM, Warner's, and 20th-Century have all guided their youthful starlets and their aging stars to Shangri-La. And it didn't take the wide, wide, world of the 7 P.M. news and the 1 A.M. talk show stars of the tube long to see that the uncapped, untinted, unbobbed, or unlifted creates a definite hazard to TV health and a threat to tubal longevity. Princess Pignatelli, the most widely known beauty of the beautiful people and a TV personality in her own right, makes no bones about how all was redone from her bunions to her eyebrows and breastline.

Though they were coming at a good clip to be siliconed, resected, sanded, tightened, loosened, or lengthened, it was a mere trickle compared to the opening of the floodgates since the Phyllis Diller phenomenon. If she could be rehabilitated, Whistler's mother could be converted into a combo of Catherine Deneuve, Cinderella, and the Mona Lisa. This miracle is in competition with those of Mother Seton, and whoever did Phyllis should be looked into by the Vatican's sainting scouts. It has given hope to many a mother and also to a horde of those thousands of dreamers who couldn't get past the doorman at Elizabeth Arden's.

The Political Preen

The biggest breakthrough for plastic surgeons—it was inevitable—were the politicians. It goes without saying, it all started with television. When the young John F. Kennedy beat Nixon in 1960, it wasn't his record, his intellect, or his ability—it was his looks. Hair tinting started when congressmen realized that their constituency was dying off and the vote went to the eighteen-year-olds. When women became interested in politics and even began to vote, tooth capping was next. The skies opened after the Proxmire press conference, when this health-bugged senator with two black eyes and a bandaged scalp came out with the fact that he had had hair plugs implanted and bags cut out from under his sagging eyes, all in the cause of Democracy. All of Washington was aghast but, used to being aghast at something or other, awaited the results. Not of the surgery but of his up-and-coming election. He won hands down and then there was a Strom, etc., etc.

Before you knew it, the plastos were doing a booming business and even old Ben Blue Mansfield was contemplating an overhaul. According to an unpublished poll, it was worth a good five to seven points on the Gallup or Harris. House Whip Tip O'Neill's beer-barrel belly could benefit from a bowel bypass, except that no research has yet been done on what that does to a fifth of Old Granddad. He could skip it though, for both Richard Daley's Chicago and O'Neill's Boston district still go for the corpulent "Tweedy" types.

Now that the debagging, implanting, and lifting business is a going thing on Capitol Hill, congressional wives aren't going to let a good thing go by. It was always tough competing with the power-struck young "Hill girls" but a touch here and a snip there puts them on a more even footing. And to be frank about it, just for the sake of an occasional male voter, Bella could stand a thorough going-over.

The Lift That Launched a Thousand Faces

Talk about the progress of vascular surgery with transplantations, or kidney surgery with dialysis, cosmetic surgery is up there with its own refinements. Gone are the days when bobbed noses looked as if they were bought wholesale and shaped by one surgeon, who somehow couldn't get that piquant little upturn to look anything like a snout. No more. It's all custom jobs made to order, only one to a customer like an original Givenchy or Balmain. *Women's Wear Daily, Vogue,* and *Silver Screen* are stacked in the waiting room so every would be beauty can pick her own combination of a Deneuve nose, Raquel Welch figure, and Jackie O. chin and cheekbones. Gone also are the days when the skin was so stretched in a face-lift that a smile was the next thing to the Risis Sardonicus of a terminal case of hydrophobia. But most important, those old tell-tale scars behind the ears are gone.

No more will their best friends have their worst fears realized by casually going behind their backs to take a look-see. Best of all in this enlightened age, a face-lift or a nose-carve is no longer a hush-hush trip to New York. Women at bridge parties trade plastic surgeons like recipes. They openly repair to the bathroom to show off how well siliconed they are amidst the oohs and ahs of their friends and compare size, shape, and lift.

Stop the Clock I Want to Stay On

As with anyone over fifty, the question always comes up, "Why not youthing instead of aging?" Why couldn't we start out saggy and wrinkled and like a good bourbon, mellow with age? Since this is beyond the pale, the next best thing is what we have—plastic surgery. But to complete the job, cosmetic geniuses are not loath to recommend those other lifters of the energy and spirit. It goes hand in glove with plasticizers, if life is to begin at seventy. Dr. Niehans of Switzerland supposedly kept Churchill, Adenauer, Toscanini, and Albert Schweitzer going until ninety. But not only were they going, but some of them chased, and made, and one actually married the nymph of his choice. The injections of embryonic lamb cells are still being dished out to the elders of Europe and the Middle East. In America we had our chance with monkey glands in the '20s and Wilhelm Reich's Orgone treatment in the '40s but turned them down.

There is another youthefying gig now in action—the lidocaine (novocaine) injectors. A Rumanian female doctor comes to Washington periodically to pump a tankload full of this innocuous stuff (it's also used for local anesthesia in drilling teeth or taking warts off)

into Washington dowagers and officials' buttocks, as
if she were cashing in wrinkles at $100 a piece. It's
had testimonials one wouldn't believe: An aging senator survived seven consecutive embassy cocktail
parties without a single misbeat of his pacemaker; one
of the Marjorie Merriweather Post set since youthefied
was seen around a Statler Hilton convention in pro-
vocative poses reminiscent of Marlene Dietrich singing
"Lili Marlene."

Straightened Genes
and Lifted Chromosomes

Plastic surgery plus youthefying is an unbeatable
combination, and what it will mean to the future of
the practice of gerontologists (doctors for the aging),
funeral directors, and the like is anybody's guess. But
it's only the beginning. The most meticulous remodel-
ing of a Sophie Tucker buttock so there is firmness
separate and equal is kid stuff compared to the genetic
plastics of the future. With the techniques soon at hand
one laser zap can clip the nasal gene in half or a few
charges of X ray in the right spots on the Titter mole-
cule of DNA and you can be sure of Marilyn Monroe
mammaries. This won't come overnight but it is in the
cards. Future mothers of America won't have to be
half-sure—they'll be able to order the baby of their
dreams through doctored genes.

Though the genetic beauty is yet to be born, the
day of the million-dollar baby is here and now, and
what with inflation, that should be the price tag for a
complete overhaul. And overhaul it is. Even now with
the crude means at hand, it's no longer piecemeal
nose, chin, or breast. The full face-and-body job is
the thing. "Oh, to be young again" is no longer an idle
wish for the idle rich. And it won't be long till every-

body's doing it, with Blue Cross and Blue Shield paying. Everything from outward youthening to inward tightening would normally be checked out in one of these unconditional all-out cases. She (and it's ten to one it's a she) will not only be able to get her man, but a progressively younger one to keep up with her backward progress every five years.

Totaled—The Million Dollar Do

For the woman who needs everything, other than the run of the mill nose job, or lift, already described, new refinements have been introduced from top to bottom. The skin of the face may be sanded or chemically peeled to a satiny finish with warts, moles, and lines obliterated and small silicone injections to give the fashionable high cheekbone look.

Heading south, the breasts are not just lifted, but minimized or maximized, pointed or blunted according to the fit and oral proclivity of the husband or boyfriend. The sag of the arms would be tucked and the lumpy cellulite of the legs made creamy smooth. Getting down to the bread basket, the old hysterectomy or gallbladder scar is eliminated and the silvery-gray pregnancy marks are sanded back to silkiness. The navel is always left and only redone if too far out or in. The next step, the pendulous abdomen, is relieved of ten pounds of fat and the muscles overlapped, giving a flat, girdleless perfection that a tree-climbing tomboy would be proud of.

Getting down to the bare bottom of things, sagging buttocks are carved to a pubertal pertness. Last but hardly least, her mate is made a most happy fella by a simple miniaturization of her most prized possession. When this major stuff is done a few days are set aside for general mop-up: bunions, liver spots, hemorrhoidal tags, or wrinkled hands.

So there you have her in all of her glory, though her own mother wouldn't know her and is probably happier for it. She's a finished if not original product right off the assembly line with no recalls at manufacturer's expense. Like a Rolls—with a refurbishing, retreading, and reupholstering every five years she can be young a lifetime.

11

Spocksmanship:
Infantilism Revisited
(Pediatrics)

If you've seen one pediatrician you've seen them all, and there's not one that isn't a pussy cat. After all, what kind of intellect opts to spend the better part of its professional life with diaper rash its most common challenge? With cowardice aforethought the baby doctor chooses to contend with an unformed, mewling, puking mass of tantrum having little brain or muscle. Rather than take his chances with the slings and arrows of outrageous adults, he opts for what he thinks is the easy way out. It's too late when he finds out he's been had.

It takes a special personality to endure the humility of chasing, needle in hand, a vicious little dynamo around the examining room and through the waiting room; or the ignominy of bursting into tears before his tiny assailant when the little chap sneakily kicks him in the most sensitive parts. And who needs the grim embarrassment of a warm, lemon-yellowish stain spreading geographically over a new summer suit as he holds the little cherub.

The pediatrician not only deliberately picks the adversary of his choice, but deals with it only through a frustrated, fear-ridden, go-between—the mother. As if this defense isn't airtight enough, he cleverly limits his contact with this proxy during "phone hours"— between 7:30 and 9 A.M. when that bedraggled creature (after those 2 and 6 A.M. feedings) is only half

human at best. With all the fight out of her, she is in
no shape to push her complaints or insist on a house
call. The rest of the day the doctor's nurse takes the
hindmost (which is literally what infant care is all
about). If by a stroke of bad fortune the emergency
strikes on nights or weekends the answering service
girl gives the benefit of her vast experience, without
charge.

Blazing Rattles

The pussycat doctor, so enamored of the new and
young, soon learns that a hot tin roof comes along
with the baby. This in turn necessitates the proverbial
nine lives and he'll use every one of them. After the
doctor's three years of training he finds, as Dr. Walt
Menninger found late in life "that they are unprinci-
pled parasites that deplete, irritate, suck, and drain
you dry."

The first hint that he should have thought twice
about his calling is his first battered-child syndrome in
the emergency room. These million broken and
bruised little things are brought in each year not by
criminals but by ordinary parents with neither a tear
in the eye nor a stricken conscience. If this doesn't
give a young baby doctor a clue to the trouble he's
in there are a dozen others that soon will. Has he
ever wondered why more and more responsible adult
women now take the pill, risking blood clots and
cancer in order to have kids less and less? Hadn't he
ever read Henry James' *The Turn of the Screw?* The
world is simply coming to its senses and seeing the
real cause of its misery. He had only to question which
families are most impoverished and which have the
most mental disease and what causes good men to
embezzle and rob? With each child, love flies further

out the window; desertion and divorce fly not too far behind.

A Mighty Hoax From Little Acorns

From a distance, the idea of not contending with the complaints and symptoms of adult neurotics is attractive, but where the young pediatrician goes wrong is imagining the child only as a soft, dimpled Bundle from Heaven, innocent and pure. Little does he know that this is only for starters; that there is a catch to it —a big catch that becomes a shock heard around the nursery. Growth! Growth, the opiate of the child, is the enemy of the adult and the scourge of the pediatrician.

Like the first-time mother who doesn't know any better, the young pediatrician completely blocks the fact that those swaddlers grow. Not only do they grow but through unimaginable phases. This isn't the worst of it—for the end, adolescence, justifies nothing, much less the means.

With each child the pediatrician goes through a psychic metamorphosis, exchanging one trauma for another. If a caterpillar with half a brain ever got a load of the rocky road from childhood to maturity it wouldn't give a fig for becoming the most beautiful butterfly on the wing. But the pediatric intern neither sees nor wants to see the bitter end, which blindness he will dearly pay for. In his original Cloud Nine euphoria, he couldn't consider the newborn as just another potential glue sniffer at the age of seven, an arsonist at thirteen, and a rapist at sixteen. No other animal species on earth goes through the outrageous process of puberty with so little appreciation for those, like the pediatrician, who only want to help.

At that crucial stage of so-called childhood the bloom is off the rose and the apparently loving, still outwardly doting pediophile doctor begins to with-draw, ultimately becoming an uptight refuge. The child has won the day. It is then that the baby doctor makes himself available only via the telephone (pref-erably from his boat). By all rights, either a child at this stage when its greatest pleasure is vandalism should be taken over by some penal institution or the pediatrician should be put out of his misery.

It's not that the young pediatrician's mentors were silent on the dangers of the garden path he was taking. They tried to warn him about the whole childhood myth, but he only chalked it up to sour grapes and future competition.

Before the die is cast, and he can back out, every medical student with a leaning toward pediatrics should have to pass English history and study Charles Dick-ens (Oliver Twist should have gotten his once and for all when he asked for that second bowl of porridge). The English in those days knew there was nothing spe-cial about kids and kids knew full well they'd better learn to take their lumps with the rest of us. This attitude brought forth superior generations that made their tiny island a conquering empire. Later, with the so-called civilizing influence of modern times, John Bull still didn't buckle under to the tot. Instead, Great Britain invented the nanny, a creature who could handle a Gila monster with one hand tied. Those were the generations which secured the empire. But then the fall. In the last few decades, they caved in to the international kiddie lobby like the rest of us and are now going down the drain with New York and Bangladesh.

Small Daft Warnings

The older pediatrician has every reason to shy away not only from the subspecies child but from the parent as well. For he knows that those selfsame maniacal parents, now tense, furtive, and given to hysterics, were once gay and even rational before that little stranger came. But together with it they make for a team the mafioso would think twice about taking on. So the doctor develops the distant proxy relationships about which the parents complain, but can do nothing.

Hearing some of these ghastly tales from broken men who have been through it (and most of their narratives are too weird or obscene to repeat in a family book of this kind), one can understand why puberty is considered the baby doctor's day of reckoning, his Yom Kippur. For here even repentance seems too late. One wouldn't believe the reports on the rapidity of aging among these specialists—many turning snow white overnight, as if they had seen Beelzebub himself. Most pediatricians under the age of forty, with the heavily furrowed, parchment-skinned faces and the woebegone look of octogenarian midgets, need no I.D. card for admission to any senior citizen project.

Pediatricians deserve some respite, if not the Medal of Freedom, for those twelve or thirteen years of servility over and beyond the call of sanity. One would think that the medical profession—or at least the local humane society—would provide some relief, some cutoff date when there could be surcease. Enough's enough. But kids, even in their teens, looking and acting like adults with social and sexual experiences adults never had (or wanted), are loath to leave such a good thing as their well baited pediatrician who gives them everything from uppers and downers to excuses from school. Some kids and parents carry it a little too far as illustrated by the case of the married man, forty-eight years old but still a thumbsucker, who still religiously goes for his three-month check-up to the same, if now senile, pediatrician to continue his uncompleted toilet training.

No other personality type in the profession would put up with it. Kids would last about one session with the surgeon before they'd be on the table and under the knife. No telling the fear the urologist or proctologist would strike in these tender hearts.

Spockwurst

Well on his way through the human sausage factory (and his ultimate fate, Spockwurst), if the pedophile were more than a pussycat, he'd just tell that thick-skinned buffer zone—the office nurse—to bar anything approaching his office with even a sprout of pubic fuzz. Other than prescribing enough sedatives to keep their wards in the twilight zone the pediatrician tries to palm off overage kids to unsuspecting colleagues. One of the more useful is the child psychiatrist. He's the only other M.D. fuzzy enough not to know what he's getting into but, at his rates, he's willing to be used. The only excuse necessary is a hint of a little incipient incest. If that doesn't work, he can always egg on the Oedipus complex, which makes every little boy or girl want to jump in bed with the parent of the opposite sex, until either mother or father have had it. The child psychiatrist who specializes in this kind of uninhibited, hyperenergized protoplasm is frequently less than the Rock of Gibraltar himself, and frequently these two disturbed humans hit it off famously—and go down together.

Speaking of Spock (or Spock-speak), most of us view this beleaguered authority on children as the prime contributor to adult fear, guilt, and neurotic collapse. He's even more prone to adult abuse than John Dewey, with the latter's advice on progressive education still sending chills up even the most liberal spine. Although Spock's claim to such ill fame for his impact on a few generations remains, he is now in the process of redemption. His slate should be wiped clean now and his salvation declared. Having sold some fifty million copies of his polemic on the care and feeding of children, the shaky results have shown that it would have been better plagiarized from *The Zookeeper's Manual on the Handling of Puff Adders*. Yet it has turned out to be the preventive medical coup of the century—though not for babies. If nothing else, it has prevented what could have been the greatest epidemic of mental breakdowns the pediatric profession has ever suffered. It was a blessing in disguise.

This little do-it-yourself paperback prevented this simply by keeping hordes of kids bottled up and out of the office. Necessity was the mother of apprehension (or mothers were the necessity for apprehension, or something). By simply advising the mother on a policy of containment of her problem to home, he foiled a minimum of 40 million office visits a year, saving the usual breakage of lamps, chairs, and typewriters, plus the general bedlamish atmosphere that is the bane of pediatric existence. The book may not have prevented one sibling from contributing disease to the next, but it certainly saved a passel of good professionals the time and expense of semiannual retreats to a place euphemistically called a rest home.

The Whole Child Catalogue

Knowing their own plight and feeling for the parent rather than the child, pediatricians now have helpful survival hints for parents—they are not loathe to prescribe tranquilizers and downers to sedate even the least hyperactive of children (if any). It was a godsend for those women wanting to get out a bit, play a little bridge, watch *Truth or Consequences* undisturbed, and pehaps have time for a clandestine little affair at home. Now they're safe, knowing the kiddies are well asleep and can neither watch nor report to daddy. It's said to have cut down on the battered-child syndrome and, given in double dose, it has saved many a parent from a child with a Lizzie Borden complex.

When the American Academy of Pediatrics was first established (there are now over 20,000 members), there was the misguided notion that a well child is less trouble-some than a sick one. Any teen-ager with a kid brother knows it's easier to handle a five-year-old with a fever of 106, depleted and dehydrated by vomiting and diar-rhea, than a well one. Even though they appear well, they are contagious carriers of disease. But the idea was too well sold to the public and the three-month well-baby visit was thus established.

The Well Baby Untouchables

Pediatricians have known for some time that those visits add less to the health of the child than to the size of his practice. Seen or unseen, the average infant is about as fragile as a brown rat. Swathed in urine and feces; kissed and pampered by adults with everything from erysipelas to pneumonia; eating dirt, coins, and insects; hanging from every conceivable fixture, window, and rooftop; and sticking every imaginable object in any bodily orifice, they take it pretty well without the benefit of that visit.

As to the reverse—a house call on something as con-tagious as a child is just courting disaster. Unless it's a life-and-death matter—or the child is absolutely well—the pediatrician never sets foot in a child ridden home.

. . . They Just Fade Away

In any event, though the pediatrician may have suc-cessfully eluded his predator on and off for many years, it is whispered about within the confines of the club that he may have overplayed his "distance makes the heart grow fonder" policy. The mothers weren't as dumb as they looked. They caught on to the greatest non-such in medical history—the pediatrician who wasn't there (you can't place the face but you recognize the phone voice). According to the gospel in *Medical Economics* entitled, "Pediatrics, The First Specialty to Go Under," the nurses are taking over—and well they might. In the article it is admitted that "few pediatricians feel competent to manage a complicated case."

Heretofore, the pediatrician has always had the nurse make the excuses, fend off the sexually aggressive, and in general do the dirty work. No more. If a nurse does an M.D.'s work she wants to get paid for it. P.N.P.s (pediatric nurse practitioners) are springing up all over, charging less and enjoying it more. So far it's been found that only 3 percent of their cases need be turned over to the pediatrician for consultation. And mothers found out that their well baby had as much disease after than before the prophylactic office visit, and that the nurse's advice wasn't half bad after all.

With this P.N.P. thing hovering over them, what do pediatricians do? It's been suggested they go into the school health or child learning field which necessitates no bodily contact. As one pediatric practitioner of twenty years said when told this, "They don't pay well enough to meet my Chris-Craft mortgage." It's also been suggested that the closest allied profession, the veterinarians, take them in, and with a little on the job training make them useful citizens again. The American Academy of Pediatricians, when backed to the wall by one of their frightened constituents, in effect said, "We're no union—if you want protection join the AMA."

It's doubtful even with all of his problems that the pediatrician will let this medicine by proxy fade away. This pussycat has always managed to land on his feet. They're not going to give up the ghost voluntarily—not even the little lethal one. Even if the child is better off, women's lib, the P.N.P., and even the mothers are going to have to fight to get rid of the baby-doctor. But mothers or mothers-to-be wherever you are, if you do, it won't change your problems with your child one bit. But remember, you won't have that pediatrician to kick around anymore.

12

The Venerable Genital:

A Phallacy

(Urology)

(This chapter may seem to dote on the vulgar and prurient but only because vulgarity and prurience is the nature of this specialty.)

The early urologists were a greater moral force for controlling a male's sexual drive than the Old Testament; and they did more for abstinence than did the priesthood. The old rack-and pincers torture was a lark in comparison to the fabled cures of the male's venereal diseases. Even today, the urologists can't escape their background: They still try to hide their shady past like a reformed old prostitute. Like Lady Macbeth, they had a hand-washing complex getting out those damned spots of Argyrol with which they irrigated corroded penises for a century.

So when the kidney stone cometh, don't expect the mores or mannerisms of the gentleman physician. The urologist was never associated with the best people or the best diseases but he was as necessary to his clientele as the bail bondsman. The sharpies, pimps, two-bit vaudeville actors, and the teen-age boys who hung around the burlesque theaters needed someone to treat their unmentionable diseases. And it was the kindly "clap doctor," as he was fondly called, who did it. His personality fit this vaudeville crowd and though not exactly one of those fallen angel types, he too had a schmaltzy heart of gold.

Since then, they've come a long way. But even now

after six or seven decades of progress, these specialists of the chancre and the discharge have had a hard time coming clean and shaking that image. Their educational background was rarely Groton and Harvard. Time was most urologists bought their M.D. degree from one of the more respected diploma mills (two hundred dollars, four weeks in school, and six weeks' apprenticeship). They could be licensed to practice in Back Bay or Park Avenue, but rarely in a hospital and never in an operating room. Though by personal preference they were drawn to the ills of the penis and though there was much poking and probing of this organ, it was a rare male who would expose his "parts" to the urologist knife—it was always the surgeon who did the cutting.

It Paid to Advertise

Urologists came into their somewhat disreputable specialty by default. After all, what respectable medical man ever looked forward to spending a lifetime with a gleety organ? However, since venereal disease was as common as the cold, it was a flourishing business. Their patients were the "high rollers" and they would pay most anything to get their most pleasure-bent organ unbent. Their recent respectability however has taken a heavy toll. (They dropped to only second in the medical income bracket; once they were number one.)

Then, they had another advantage, for they believed it paid to advertise. This was before the AMA got so finicky about it. So the burlesque theaters and houses of ill-repute had neat professional cards tacked in the wash room (mainly above the urinals):

Men's Diseases Only
Confidential
121 Fleet St.—above Selig's Pawnshop

Every druggist had a stack of these cards (with a 50 percent kickback in the offing) for all of the kids in the neighborhood who "caught it off of toilet seats"—and for the special clientele uptown, "by appointment only." The flyspecked and somewhat gamy-odored offices were for some reason always one steep flight up, usually in run-down theater districts not far from the source of their business, the two-dollar house. The high and mighty sat alongside the tout picking his teeth and reading the *Police Gazette,* both waiting for their moment of truth. That weekly Argyrol injection, and the urinating trial by fire that followed the rod of steel, made both prince and pauper come away weak-kneed and goggle-eyed.

Sin, Syph, Sulfa, and Cystoscopes

Before penicillin, urologists were also irrevocably linked with syphilis, for after diagnosis the neighborhood doctor would never let "it" contaminate his homey office. When the chancre or secondary spots appeared, it was down to the friendly second-story man and off to a life of more sin. For this was the dread disease that every doctor knew drove one to the booby hatch more surely than masturbation. The treatment consisted of Salvarsan or Ehrlich's silver bullet (606) and, as the moralists intoned, "One night with Venus and three years with Mercury."

But that's all finished now. In the '30s and '40s sulfa drugs and penicillin not only brought the urologists up out of the shadowy era of syph and clap but down from his second-floor aerie and bathroom advertising to the legitimacy of the Medical Arts Buildings and the hospital.

As time went on, the old-time clap doctor did develop a certain expertise in the manipulation of sounds and scopes in the organ of his choice. But the operating room and the knife were still off-limits. One couldn't expect a specialist who spent a century with "unspeakable diseases of the privates" to become a respected man in white overnight. They finally made it into the sterile white sanctum sanctorum of high fees but only the hard way—literally working their way up the penis. Proceeding step by step, it was first up the canal to the old man's burden, the prostate. Then into the bladder with its stones by way of the male animal's nightmare—the cystoscope. From there, they gradually ascended both ureters against the stream to reach the medical respectability of a real working organ, the kidney.

So the urologist's star rose via the cystoscope. With new pipe-cleaning and sewer-unclogging procedures he then became an expert at faulty kidney tubes, clogged penis drains, and damaged bladder receptacles. Though the glamor of his theater and circus clientele went out with antibiotics, the down-to-earth respectability of the dues-paying member of the steam-fitters union were now his. Strangely enough, he seemed to have a technical bent in that direction; as one watched him snare a stone from the bladder, it brought to mind the plumber fishing the baby's teething ring out of the bowl.

If anything helped the urologist climb his fluid ladder to success it was the common kidney stone. The pain of that pinhead bit of gravel "coming through the rye" made Christians of many an infidel. It can only be compared to being in labor while suffering from gangrenous hemorrhoids complicated by a cigarette cough. One shot of morphine and a devout believer was made for life. Only the relief of such misery—when the stone is passed or removed—could account for the urologist's phenomenal fees. At the turn of the century Diamond Jim Brady gave urologic institutes to his surgeons in both Baltimore and New York in grateful appreciation. Few other ailments helped the urologist to stardom and wealth like the stone—yet he still has no more idea of why they form or how to prevent them than he did a century ago.

The Pageantry of Gadgetry

As with most of medicine, first there's the bad news. In poking into the penis and bladder with his shiny chrome tube, the uro caused more chills, fever, and lethal blood poisoning than a bushelful of the stones he grappled for. Cystoscopy has been the cause of more deaths than the once lethal operation, the prostatectomy. But it fazed him little, for he was the engineering type, knowledgeable about the hydraulics of an obstructed bladder but a little vague on the germ theory of disease. He is also not too strong on physiology, knowing less about the artificial kidney than Isaac Stern knows about handling a cystoscope.

But now the good news. With the antibiotics and other injections that put gonorrhea back into the lap of the G.P., the urologist almost (but not quite) lost his clap-doctor image. He began plumbing by day and plumbing by night, inserting any number of tubes and catheters into the bladder, squirting dyes into the kidneys, and—lo and behold—the patients survived, some even without infection. He then went into his gadget period, which he's never really come out of, inventing more electric and optical gimcrackery than Thomas Edison and Marconi together.

At this stage in his history, the urine-specialist physician, having seen what he could get away with using a blunt instrument, got up his nerve and began toying with a sharp one. Self-trained in the use of the scalpel, he roamed the territory he'd already staked out for himself from penis to kidney with about the refinement of the abattoir. His results were sometimes astounding, with urine seeping from every orifice except the right one and creating medical curiosities unheard of in urologic annals.

The Greening of the Prostate

But in a matter of a few decades things settled down and as the general surgeon found his appendix and the neurosurgeon his disc, the urologist found his pot at the end of the penis—the prostate. One never would have thought that the tough rubbery little organ about the size and consistency of a quince, through whose portals pass the most golden urine and the most platinum ejaculate in the world, would open new vistas for the old-time clap doctor. What's more, the urologist found that this organ was doubly blessed—for as it bulged with age, so did the patient's bank account, and as it shut off his water, he became even more amenable to sharing his wealth with his savior.

As in every age and every specialty there is a medical messiah. For the aged and the stopped-up, it was Dr. Hugh Young. He was the same charming, ambitious young doctor who fixed old Diamond Jim Brady by removing a stone from his ureter. Brady, as Lillian Russell's boyfriend, was deadly afraid of the current myth that the urologist's knife would also cut his "potency nerve." Young obviously killed two birds with that one stone, leaving Jim's virility intact. After all, no matter how many diamonds he had, one doesn't leave whole institutes to a half-baked doctor just for turning half his water back on.

In any event Young conned this tycoon into donating to the Johns Hopkins the Brady Institute, which still stands as a "stone" monument. But Hugh Young went on to an even more lucrative field. This famous pioneer took that little gland, overlooked for centuries, except for weekly rituals of the elderly's painful massage, and turned it into a golden egg. Almost single-handedly he brought urology from the nickel-and-dime game of treating tarts and pimps, to milking the plugged-up millionaires for all they were worth. He made that organ, once accused of enlarging because old men sat on cold stoops, a household word by inventing a brand-new super-scientific unclogging operation. It was no big deal and it's hardly done anymore but it was an improvement (though barely) over crudely shelling it out like an onion with the finger through the opened bladder. Most of all, patients didn't need to deplete the Red Cross blood bank to survive. It had a few drawbacks, such as infection, months of leaking, and even impotence. But it was Young's baby and he sold it from Hollywood to Timbukto. Prostated European royalty and Latin American dictators dribbled their way back to their castles and haciendas, happy and content, bereft of prostates and fortunes alike with an arc that could once again clear the chicken house as in their boyhood days.

But this operation wasn't so popular among those unlucky Latin macho types who got back only to find that the old gray bear wasn't what he used to be. So even this less than perfect operation inspired improvement. For they then put a little blade on the end of the cystoscope, and can now ream out five prostates a day, leaving the blood bank intact, with no need to defend themselves from the irate male animals furious at their lost manhood.

The Uro-jock

Dr. Young set the style not only in the operating room but also in the barroom. Those who have since fit into his shoes seem to follow the leader not only in techniques and gigantic fees but also in style. The urologic conventions under Dr. Young's leadership could only have been equaled by Henry VIII in his prime. Those bacchanalias of booze and gluttony, with girls jumping out of pies and into beds all in the guise of science and humanity, have been the envy of every pious internist and inhibited cardiologist.

As the word got around, it was probably the greatest bait in recruiting urologic interns. The meetings in between (especially in the darkness of a slide demonstration) for giving learned (learned?) papers were mainly a mid-day respite needed for relief and recuperation so they could be fresh for another go at it come the first taste of the juice of the juniper. Hugh Young himself led the parade.

The new breed of urologic specialists is no doubt different, but not that different. They're still drawn by the same old penile fixation. Superimposed is a thin veneer of sophistication and pseudo-science, yet they're still perplexed by the kidney's conversion of booze and beer into urine. At least nowadays their clothes are not stained, and they no longer emanate the aroma of the washroom at the Bijou. Their surgical techniques are still more the cleaving and rending of the stockyards than the detailed meticulousness of a neurosurgeon. They are still deadly afraid of mistakenly breaking into the abdominal cavity or cutting into the bowel—hopefully there is always a real surgeon on standby. Though they may operate on a prostate of anyone over fifty who looks cross-eyed at a bathroom after 9 P.M., it's harder to pin unnecessary surgery on them than on a psychiatrist.

Even between conventions, life is not dull in the urologic bathysphere. If complications and weird happenings occur in any specialty, it's in this one. But one as used to operative complications as the urologist doesn't dilate a nostril when a patient urinates from the weirdest places or ejaculates from a region that could never propagate the race. And more objects, from Eversharps to bobby pins, have been extracted from the bladder

than the usual nuts, bolts, and coins discovered by X-ray
in the stomach.

Hardened Arteries and Fallen Appendages

At one time, other than treating the king's festering
privates and giving him a special concoction for his
waning manhood, one of the urologist's special if routine
duties was the creation of eunuchs. Both the master's
harem and his church choir depended on it. But that
was long before the scientists let the urologists in on the
fact that "thar's gold in them thar orbs." Since then, he
handles them as *genitally* as if they were truly the golden
eggs of the male goose—which of course, they are. What
else—being the seat of his sperm, his macho, and the
origin of his zest and libido? The precious testosterone
therein encased has now elevated the run-of-the-mill
uro far above the murky waters of his urinal pursuits.
Though those precious hangings are his only by prox-
imity, he's made the most of them. With the instinct
he was born with, plus a smattering of endocrinology
gleaned from his yearly subscription to the *Reader's
Digest,* he dispenses advice to the love-shorn and hormones for the reborn with doubtful results and un-
doubted financial rewards. Masters and Johnson tried
to cut in on the male virility game with the flimsy argu-
ment that both male and female must be treated together. But the hardening of the male's arteries, which
causes the fall of his principal appendage, brings him
to the urologist first—and there he stays.

The urologist treats every sexual inadequacy from
premature ejaculation to no ejaculation at all with that
elixir of life worth living, testosterone. Though not sub-
stituting for hormones, he's found that his average patient at fifty to ninety responds better to a change of female venue and menu. He not infrequently advises his

male clients to this effect, and has not been loath to recommend a female Rx. With hope springing eternal, even if none of this works, the therapy lingers on.

Now there's even a new wrinkle (or unwrinkle) to that age-old problem. It sounds brutal but it works. It is, of all things, the same as the answer to the flat-chested maiden's prayer—silicone! By inserting a magic silicone rod into the tissue of the penis it makes the most hangdog member a proud possession. There are a few medical complications to this one-shot injection but these are nothing compared to its difficult social side effects. The problem is that from the insertion evermore, the penis is all upbeat—with no let down. It not only poses a tailoring problem depending on the natural endowment but can even be embarrassing when standing around at cocktail parties or with the preacher after church, not to mention when attired for tennis or swimming.

As many-faceted as the urologist's work seems to be, it is neither intellectually demanding, meticulous in nature, nor physically strenuous. There is a certain flexibility and adaptability inherent in his character. He's shown it, he easily shifted from life as a second-story man to a quasi-respectable member of the medical fraternity; then from the organic ills of the penis in the young all the way to the psychic ills in the heads of the old. Luckily he has few real medical decisions to make, as the major illnesses of the kidney itself are taken care of by those who understand physiology better than plumbing. In essence he's a simple man with simple tastes in a simple cut-and-dried business, tending the easiest, least complaining of the sexes and is generally a most happy, healthy, and wealthy fella.

13

The Disposables:

The Lucrative Fringe

(Proctologists, Allergists, Dermatologists, Nose and Throat, etc.)

Like anything else in the throw-away era of modern medicine, even some specialties may be disposable. There are specialists and there are specialists; then there are the ones who've spent almost half of their lives learning about disease and the rest avoiding it. One would think after going through ten to thirteen years of learning and training, a physician would want to spend the rest of his life doing something more useful than mulling over dandruff scrapings. And what kind of intellect does it take to match wits with an itching anus. Why didn't the dermatologists, the allergists, proctologists, and their fellow travelers who hang around the fringes of the healing art choose an easier avocation with less preparation and headaches, like used-car dealing?

But who knows? A fringer like the dermatologist might not have been able to tell the difference between poison ivy and prickly heat without those years at the cadaver, microscope, and stethoscope. Maybe it takes that to prescribe patent medicines, ointments, and lotions for scabies and chiggers. It just seems to those not trained in the sciences that the eleven years and eight months of preparation could have been spent better studying the Dow Jones charts.

The fringers charge high; but, unlike the G.P. or the gynecologist, their volume is low and they must make ends meet. Yet with what they get for what they give, one would think their ends meet so well they may over-shoot. Even the more erudite fringers like the gastro-enterologists are expensive, though their whole schmier revolves around a pinch of baking soda before and after each meal.

The Heeler Dealers

Is there a wise old grandmother anywhere who couldn't have taken care of all of those sore throats, gassy stomachs, and tired blood between doing the housework, painting the living room, and making a pie? Calling some of them specialists is a slap in the face to the tribal medicine man who may have started it all when he would limit exorcising succubi from only the right eardrum or the left nostril. The nose and throater (or otolaryngologist, as he likes to be called) is a case in point. No question they prescribe gargles that may do a neat trick on a sore throat, but the Listerine doctor on TV doesn't do badly either. The allergist is another. Lord knows what a nose-blowing victim of hay fever gets out of him, except antihista-mines that make him too sleepy to sneeze.

We know all this and we know equally well why those little specialist boutiques have sprung up. If the American public thought they had to pay extra for this out of their own pockets, instead of through an insur-ance company's, they'd never bother. They'd normally wait for it to go away or put their eyes to better use reading *Doctor Ziegenfoose's Home Doctoring Book*.

The Puckered Patch Practitioner

The proctologist (the rectal specialist) is a typical lucrative fringer. It's debatable whether he must know all the scientific facts about the location of the pancreas or the working of the pituitary gland, or the function of the facial nerves when 90 percent of the complaints he hears come from one square inch of the body surface.

Maybe one day it'll all come in handy as with the urologist, who once treated only the penis and now has gone right up to the kidney. It's not that he hasn't tried to improve himself by social climbing into the more socially acceptable reaches of the rectum, but at that point he finds his way solidly blocked by the gastro-enterologist and the general surgeon. They stand firmly at the large bowel's Maginot Line where the rectum joins the lower colon, declaring, "He shall not pass."

Both of these more respected specialists look down their bowel at the proctologist as some sort of opportunistic untouchable who has neither the brains nor the skill to treat anything but his small puckered patch. This down grading of the anus doctor is undeserved since his proud history is anything but undistinguished. It seems that a certain select coterie of orificial compulsives have always been fascinated by the lowliest of body exits. For many years their most scientific form of therapy was the enema. On the surface this may sound home-remedyish, but these early specialists showed great creativity in their art and had results that compare favorably with those of today.

The Enema of Man

Proctologists were much more romantic and roving then. It may have been rectum first, rectum last, and rectum always (with impeccable rectitude), but through that hollow tube they treated some of the most exotic of bodily illnesses. Enemas had a more elegant name in those times and were thus much more acceptable as a therapy. They were called clysters and they were well utilized not only for simple constipation, but for serious illness: Fevers, vapors, faintings, and gout.

The means of their administration were wondrous to behold and not the willy-nilly five-minute spritz they are today. It was done thoroughly, with exquisite attention to details such as ingredients, amounts, and temperature. Frequently these clysters, with as much as five gallons of liquid (only two are used by veterinarians on a sick cow), had to be retained overnight. This, of course, said something for either the physical and mental endurance of the patient of that day, or they had the colon of a dray horse.

Some of the more successful clysters were the soothing type with milk, oil, and honey for paranoia; others with beer and cider tended to have a pleasant after-effect. Those with ox brain were a catchall sort of thing. There were also special clysters for certain diseases, such as the wine enema for tuberculosis (a Burgundy '94—1394, that is—was supposedly an excellent year). Tobacco-smoke clysters for hernias, to our more modern scientific minds, seem a little far-fetched (it's still unknown how this was done). One of the more interesting proctologic gambits into the spiritual realm was the holy-water enemas (brought to a boil first) which supposedly exorcised more devils from possessed nuns than all the Inquisitors in Spain.

It's only been a few years since a Dr. Gerston from Florida prescribed enemas every two hours for weeks as a sure cure for all kinds of cancer. This was dutifully entered into the congressional record by a congressman high on a health subcommittee. It would have gotten much further if the mortality from inundation hadn't been as high as the deaths from the disease.

The proctologist first entered the surgical field during the Renaissance when the application of leeches was in its prime. One of the top royal researchers found that a leech applied at the anus was worth two on the scrotum. Since the proctologist started bleeding with the leech, it was also up to him to stop it before the patient was totally depleted. He did so by putting a few sutures in. By this sort of scientific serendipity, he was well on his way to devising the classic hemorrhoidectomy.

Though there's nothing wrong with enema therapy, surgery of the nether region took hold early. Proctology is no different from any other specialty—if you use the knife, you cut the ice. Varicose veins of the anus are rarely lethal and the ordinary sitz bath with a little Epsom salts and a few days of patience usually does the trick. But what kind of Rx is that for a specialist with all of that training? If hemorrhoidectomy weren't part of his repertoire how could he hold his head high with other fringe specialists?

It's Alimentary Dear Watson

With the gastroenterologist, another specialist of an alimentary nature, it's a whole other story. He has the distinction of being the great nonspecialist of all quasi-specialties. Gastroenterologists encompass all twenty-nine feet of the dimly lit gastrointestinal (G.I.) world from the germ-infested gullet to the very end.

Between the various scopes they use, plus the barium meals, barium enemas, and X rays, they roam the entrails with more theories than success. Since the X ray is in the hands and billing of others, their scoping is charged by the inch to make up for it. For instance: up to the rectum $100; the lower reaches of the colon $150; and, since the Japanese invented the new flexible scope, the higher colon $300. From the other end, their price list goes from an esophagus at $100 to a tough duodenum at $250, with the stomach at a price somewhere in between.

Other than an occasional bit of regurgitated gastric juice on their white starched lab coats, the G.I. man's person remains as clean as his diagnostic record. Most of the diseases are a matter of philosophy to him, for they are diagnosed by X ray and treated by surgeons. There are only two classes of disease which he claims solely as his own. Both of these, the common garden variety of stomach or duodenal ulcer and ileitis and colitis, come to him only when they become so chronic that neither surgeon nor internist can or wishes to handle them any longer. Of course (as with practically any other ills of the flesh), the psychiatrist has also laid claim to these as being within the psychosomatic sphere of influence.

The gastroenterologist is supposedly the expert, or at least the last word, on the other organs which empty into his convoluted domain. Of those, the gallbladder (just a receptacle for bile) is strictly surgical. The pancreas well or ill is a total mystery to him as well as to every other doctor. The liver, which forms the bile, he inundates with dyes and punches with needles (occasionally fatal) to little diagnostic avail. Hepatitis, both natural or hospital-induced, is as foggy to the G.I. man as to the host of other doctors.

As the G.I. man fends off the psychs, the surgeon, and even the lowly proctologist, he's on the lookout for other fields to conquer. He has even tried to squeeze in on the diet game. But how can a legit professorial type, with neither guile nor guts, come off against the show-biz Stillmans or the Solomons with their wonder diets. He has done his best (which is none too good) with ileitis, but a surgeon had to cure Eisenhower. The G.I.'er has played with enzymes, toyed with hormones, and tagged radioisotopes to little avail.

So he has little left as he wanders the hospital corridors, searching under every bed sheet for a new disease he can spot. Until some lucky break he must depend on the ulcer, of which he still knows neither the cause nor the cure. In every medical journal there's a treatment of the month for ulcers ranging from hashish malteds to an old Chinese almond remedy. Though there have been no controlled series, it is bruited about in family doctor circles that Alka-Seltzer and its cheaper version, baking soda, do just as well, which isn't saying an awful lot even for baking soda.

The Consul of the Tonsil

Though the 4,000 gastroenterologists in search of a disease may not have found their El Dorado, they've never resorted to make-work like the nose and throat man. This specialist can point to a hundred diseases from otosclerosis to nasopharyngotracheitis as being among the many he must diagnose and treat. But anyway he slices it, the sum and substance of his specialty has been and still is tonsils, tonsils, and more tonsils.

Each year, a million and a half of those little devils that actually harm no one are trouped through the operating rooms. (Laid end to end the yearly take would reach from New York to Trenton, New Jersey.)

Though it's certain a tonsillectomy rarely helps the throat (or cures arthritis), it's a sort of ritual, like circumcision among the Bantus when they come of age. The only thing is that the Bantus do it a little later in life and seem to come out of it better. By the skillful hand of the nose and throater only about 300,000 of our young warriors get any complications at all, and fewer than 140 die in this annual refining process.

Tonsillectomy is done for everything but tonsillitis (no nose and throat man will touch a tonsil if it's inflamed; a half-dozen antibiotic capsules work better), and though no known cure of anything has ever been proved by it, the E.N.T. man has a case. In all fairness, since the tonsil is easily available, can be seen with the naked eye, and is of questionable utility, why not remove it? Also three or four of them can be removed in an hour if the assembly line is working, which leaves this specialist free for other scientific pursuits the rest of the day. Then again mothers are already sold on the operation and the diseases it might prevent, so why rock the boat?

What You Don't Have Won't Hurt You

Actually the tonsillectomy became a way of life when it was brought to America after World War I. The army doctors overseas saw what a going thing it was in the old Austro-Hungarian empire and couldn't resist bringing this panacea over for the good of all Americans. So in the '20s, as soon as the diploma was in hand every would-be nose and throat specialist made a beeline to Vienna. There for a month or two he guzzled Löwenbräu and muzzled Sacher Torts, spending an hour or so daily in the *Krankenhaus* learning the Tonsil and Adenoid game. On return, it helped them pass their E.N.T. boards, which were brand-new at the time.

Recently, because of the bad-mouthing the T and A got from the salaried professors who don't know a good thing when they see it, a few of the more timorous nose and throat men are cutting down. They've been intimidated by the claim that of the million and a half yearly tonsillectomies, a million and a half are unnecessary. This is a gross exaggeration: studies have shown that about 30,000 really should have been done.

The big T is no doubt the main event but it shouldn't be thought that nose and throat is a Johnny-One-Note specialty. For an enterprising young man with an eye to specialize (and no special affinity) for work, there are other interesting tidbits to break the monotony. Sucking out sinuses or testing for deafness are not child's play and an occasional deviated septum that has slipped through the fingers of the plastic man is as mean a challenge as flushing out a stuffy ear passage.

The Skin Game

It's peculiar how a morbid disease like syphilis once came under a specialty whose most powerful medication was calamine lotion for the pimply skin of adolescents. Because the chancre usually started on the skin of the penis, with a secondary breaking out, the skin man was saddled also with the later effects of paresis, blindness, and madness, which he not only knew nothing about but was too frightened to deal with. Later on, when simpler skin ailments like acne and the hundreds of legitimate lesions from industry came his way, he would hide, disguise his voice over the telephone, and even wear a fake moustache to get out of the office without a syphilitic spotting him.

It's not that he's timid. It's only a cliché that the reason an M.D. goes into the skin game is that there are no cures, no kills, and no night calls. Although penicillin put venereal diseases outside of his ken, he still had other risky things to deal with, such as pubic lice (crabs). However anyone who thinks there are no emergencies with this rather sedentary specialty should know the panic of a post-pubescent boy with his first post-prostitute case of crabs, the hush-hush visits, and the embarrassing soiling of clothes by the conventional blue ointment treatment.

Other than those major problems, dermatology is as handy a dodge as there is in medicine and not one we could very well do without. To whom else could an octogenarian female with an epidermis like parchment go for advice on which lotions, creams, hormones, and packs to use to return it to its original lushness? In the privacy of their offices dermatologists also turn their hand to a little surreptitious surgery with warts and one-stitcher biopsies of moles at twenty-five to fifty dollars a throw. They also look terribly professional with their magnifying binoculars as they wax scientific, taking dandruff scrapings to see whether the case should be treated by Head and Shoulders or Halo.

But as usual, there is one fly in the unguent. Besides acne, which they've given up on, psoriasis, the most common, unsightly, but wholly legitimate disease they see, can't be cured. They've tried everything from turtle wax to yoga and they're as stumped on its cause as its cure. Even their very own miracle drug—cortisone ointment, which can erase practically any eruption that will eventually disappear on its own—can't lay a glove on psoriasis.

Ka-choo!!

Other than the plastic surgeon, who's taken over the job of youthefying the skin, the only competitor of the dermatologist is the allergist. He's not really a competitor; it's only that their work overlaps, and frequently it comes down to a fielder's choice—whoever gets there first treats it. For instance, hives is allergic—but it complicates things by showing up in the skin. So the skin man who is stumped by just about everything that isn't erased overnight by C.C. (not Canadian Club—calamine and cortisone), sends it posthaste to the closest specialty just in case.

The funny thing about immunology, as it's called in the profession, is that it's as mysterious to the average doctor or patient as electricity or radio. There's nothing a good down-to-earth healer can either see under the microscope or cut out.

Gesundheit!

Though the allergist started out very seriously with Jenner and his vaccination for an epidemic disease like smallpox, its most serious problem today is the sneeze. Grown men have spent a lifetime in this pursuit with less than rave results. Hay fever is to the allergist what the hysterectomy is to the gyno. The only difference is that we know that hay fever does indeed cause a lot of misery. But before a cure is even contemplated there is a routine trial by needle whereby a sneezer is tested over a period of months for everything that man can possibly breathe, touch, or ingest. When the cause is finally narrowed down to an even dozen (from mother's milk to the baby's touch), the yearly series of injections begin. Everything from an extract of chair leg to a concoction of termite wings is put back into the patient through a series of needle pricks. If none of this works, the next best thing is a finger held securely under the nose.

Another rather common immunologic disease, asthma, can hardly be pried loose from the family doctor, internist, or pediatrician. Until there's trouble that can't be overcome by a Vicks inhaler, or the patient needs adrenaline right into the heart, the primary doctor (the one who gets there first) holds on tight. The family doctor knows that once a patient gets the first needle prick from the allergist, he's like a junky, and out of his clutches forever. As the psychs put it, they develop a dependency.

Allergists, like all other fringe specialties, are not averse to poaching on a colleague's territory. Immunologists like Dr. Good at the Sloan-Kettering Institute are trying to put tumors into the hay fever category even though they don't sneeze. They are testing and treating bladder cancers and leukemia by their little needle-prick techniques. As usual when someone thinks he is onto something big like curing the now incurable (and they do have a pretty good record with measles, chicken pox, typhoid, and such) there are a few Yahoos who want stardom. This happened to the good Dr. Good when one of his experimenters came up with the breakthrough (it's always a breakthrough). Then when a few things went wrong, he had to admit that his star struck experimenter had committed a hoax. (Since it wasn't breaking and entering or arson the man was sent to a psych rather than jail.)

There are a passel of potential fringe freak physicians who are also doing very nicely with a minimum of work and a maximum of—well, whatever the patient will buy. There are the endocrinologists, befuddled by hormones, trying by injection to get midget kids to start growing and giant kids to stop growing and there are others with outstretched palms who do nothing but hand surgery. Then there are the superfringers waiting patiently in the wings. If the syphilologist, the diabetician, the arthrologist, and the pedioschiziac (a child psychiatrist only doing schizoid kids) are here already, can the herpes zosterite, and the pruritis vulverat be far behind? To extend this all the way, if there is a pediatrician and a gerontologist, why not a prepubertologist, an adolescentist (ugh!), and even a singlist and a marriologist. On and on it will go ad infinitum, all doing less and less for more and more according to Parkinson's law and the Peter Principle, till the American Board of Blackhead Specialists convenes for its first international convention.

14

The Hip Bone's Connected to the Thigh Bone:

The Fractured Franchise

(Orthopedics)

Any M.D. who has to worry about his tax bracket after only six months in practice is a folk hero to his peers. In medicine, only the orthopod can claim this distinction. From the opening bell lawyers, chronics, hop heads, and the accident prone are lined up six deep for his services—his X ray and billing computer clicking. Get rich quick Mulligan had nothing on the orthopod. He's admitted to the golden circle in record time, even before the gynecologist. And if the legal and insurance angles aren't pushed to extremes, it's all semi-legitimate.

Some reasons for this instant success are obvious. As a student, the orthopod was one of the few with enough muscular heft to carry the little black bag for a reasonable time without fatigue. Then, as the only jock in the profession, he can at least handle bone setting without the benefit of block, tackle, or winch. Secondly, most doctors are so unmechanical they have trouble getting the new safety tops off an aspirin bottle. But it's mainly a big money maker because it's just another symptom wastebasket, like psychiatry. Since the body is over 80 percent bone, muscle, and fiber, every ache, pain, or charley horse that isn't in the skull or abdomen makes the first stop at the orthopods'. This well-muscled dispose-all with his X ray, diathermy, and physiotherapists makes the most of it.

Proudly calling itself the work horse of the profession, this specialty bounces busily back and forth from the plaster room, to the emergency room, to the court room. The orthopedist is another of those specialists who could have skipped all but a year or so of medical school and internship. Why should he, who won't in his entire career see the inside of the body, worry about all of those complicated anatomical parts when his only interest will be in the skeleton and what makes it move. Even diseases within his bone and joint bailiwick (like arthritis) are *verboten*. (In fact a new fringe freak has just been anointed—the arthologist—for joints only.)

Anything that can't be seen by X ray, cured by aspirin and bed rest, or put in a cast is strictly off limits. In their training the orthopods could have been better apprenticed to carpenters or plasterers. Almost everything they treat they either splint, screw, nail, or brace. They're a little ashamed of this blue collar image but still use more plaster in a year than the average small construction company.

The First National Bone Bank

The modern orthopedist gets to know the ropes in short order. Before he sets his first bone or shoots his first syringe of cortisone into a tennis elbow, the legal minds have shown him the ins and outs of obscuring facts, coddling the malingerer and jacking up the disability. The chronics with their low back pains and even more vague muscle pulls, having run out of last year's crop of orthopods, will be there in force to give the new man a trial run.

By this time, the ortho has hired his physiotherapist and technicians and has already gone for over seventy-five thousand dollars' worth of equipment, adding another fifty thousand for a computer to make sure that the first seventy-five gets paid off. Immediately his waiting period for an appointment is twenty-seven days. He then begins to hire help like the Alaskan pipeline. And each and every one he puts on the rolls will pay off just as well as his diathermy machine or his whirlpool. In ten days a physiotherapist earns his keep for the month—after all, what sprained ankle or pulled muscle doesn't need a little organized exercise to bring it back in shape? Two more X ray technicians can have the machines going round the clock and doubling up the secretaries can get the forms back to the insurance companies before the patient leaves the office. In one new orthopedic corporation in Boston there are only three surgeons. They have their formal board meetings each month, complete with agendas on stock options, policy statements, overtime pay, Christmas bonuses, and incentive awards for their twenty secretaries and technicians. Of the twenty, eighteen are busy filling out forms, directing traffic or listening to complaints the doctors are too busy for.

The Aching Back Annuity

Though the Lord in his even-handedness distributes his heavenly largesse to every specialist—unusual noses for the plastos, hives for the allergos or acne for the dermos—the orthos are no doubt the chosen people. To them He has granted that golden complaint—the aching back, which puts even the tonsil to shame. The thought of being the receiver for the multitudinous aches and pains of some 290 muscles, bones, and joints from the base of the skull to the anal coccyx gives them that old Fort Knox feeling. Even that spin off, the disc (which they begrudgingly gave over to the neuro—after a twenty year squabble) is milked dry with X ray and traction by the orthopod before it's referred on. Multiply the potential number of symptoms from 290 separate pieces of back that could (and do) go wrong by the number of visits for each (plus the charges for the extra addeds of massage, heat, and rays) for the 25 million people who suffer it—and they've got a king's ransom, even if they never set another leg. One low back problem, beginning from a number 2 iron swing on the water hole on a damp autumn morning, can last a lifetime and cost a fortune, not counting the aspirin investment.

Autodeedee and Cycledeedum

But the bone jock needn't depend on the back alone. He's not only blessed but triply so. The second mother lode came into being with the automobile. The orthopedic association keeps up with automobile production and imports just like any Chrysler or General Motors executive.

> Sticks and stones will break their bones
> But autos do it faster

It's been figured out mathematically that every new car on the highway is good for a minimum of two cases every five years, averaging three to four fractures (there are 125 million cars and trucks on the road). "Autos are a pod's best friend" and the more flimsy the imported ones the better.

More recently, in the finest hara-kiri tradition, the Japanese have come forth with an instant daredevil campaign, putting motorcycles under the seat and guidance of every suicide-prone kid from age six to thirty (incidentally developing one of the best sources for heart transplants). Some malicious wags have suggested that the largest stockholders in Yamaha, Honda, and Kawasaki industries are orthopedic surgeons. Bone for bone, the orthopod wouldn't trade a Yamaha 900 cycle for three paper thin Volkswagens or ten Chryslers.

If the American Society of Orthopedic Surgeons had tried, they couldn't have invented an Evel Knievel. With fifty broken bones already under (or over) his belt, he has converted enough kids to cycledom to assure standing room only in emergency rooms for the next five years. If he ever wants sponsors for another Snake River enterprise he knows where to find them. This great American can go anywhere in the world and get splinted, braced, and casted for free.

Until the cycle fad was brought back from the old Harley-Davidson days (with skiing for the off-season), the orthopod spent only one-third of his time in the emergency room. Now he's had to sharply cut down on his court time in order to put together all the pieces brought in from the road.

The Doctor In-law

The modern orthopedic surgeons (especially those legally oriented) know more about mandamesis and parties of the third part than they do about fallen metatarsal arches and trick knees. It is questionable whether any lawyer in the land spends more time before the bar than the orthopedist (or the psychiatrist —with the orthos now pulling ahead). Bone surgeons are in court so frequently that if the judge gets stuck on some point of law, the orthopod can always be quietly called to the chambers to help straighten it out. Being on such mutually respectful terms, when the judge hands down his disability verdicts it's only natural the doctors get the best of it.

But the orthopod has experience on both sides of the fence. He is not only trained to do his best for his lawyer's clients but he ranks with the gynecologist and the neurosurgeon when it comes to malpractice suits. So he has become an authority on court tactics for the whole of medicine. He has developed several classical examples of defense for malpractice suits and has created evasive tactics in his own defense so perfect (even after causing paralysis on a disc case or gangrene after an artery is cut) that even psychiatrists seek his legal council.

Most negligence lawyers wouldn't be caught dead in court without their bone doctor by their side. If a worker hurt his back lifting a paper crate in a powder puff factory and the court's Ivory Tower consultant says the disability is between one and one-half percent, the lawyer's orthopedist automatically claims total disability, as the patient is wheeled into court on a stretcher. What this patient can do in the neighborhood bowling alleys or the connubial bedroom is none of the court's business and would involve invasion of privacy. At worst, court compromises bring in about 40 percent of what's claimed, which isn't bad for the lawyer or the brotherly bone crusher.

Whittler's Mother

But the orthopod's life isn't all courts, casts, and sacroiliacs. They are also charter members in good standing of the Guild of the Razor's edge. In ancient times the orthopedist earned his soubriquet of sawbones by amputating gangrenous arms or legs when not employed in carving out sides of beef. Even then his abattoir was in hopping distance to his subcontractor (the prosthetic expert of the day), the whittler of the peg leg. "Off with it," was his motto in those days and business was brisk. Though a few centuries have passed since Captain Hook, Ahab, and Long John Silver showed up as shining examples of orthopedic handiwork, amputation has not lost its traditional lure to the bone doctors. Frequently it's only taking care of problems they create themselves with a severed artery, a tight cast, or a bone infection. One of the best publicized cases in malpractice against a hospital, one that couldn't be covered up or settled out of court, was an amputation necessitated by a constricting cast (which, by the way, has boosted malpractice premiums for hospitals some 2000 percent).

Though orthos spend most of their workhorse hours in the accident room they are wending their way into the OR, as they see the respect it draws from their medical peers and patients. They are gradually introducing more and more procedures that can be done only there.

Recently they're on a joint kick (not the smoking kind). Why creak, they ask, when a new plastic and chrome hip can give you a glide like Fred Astaire? They've also seen the error of just straightening a fracture and putting on a plastic cast when pinning, screwing, or plating it in the operating room offers better results for the ortho—if not always the patient.

The Ortho's Complaint

As blessed as they are, orthopedics get no free ride. Talk about the internecine problems between the various medical specialties, the orthopods have them all. Not only do the plastic surgeons object to their lengthening and shortening jobs but the vascular and general surgeons want more of the amputation action, the neurosurgeons have already wrestled the disc away from most of them, the podiatrists have sneaked in and filched fallen arches and flat feet, and the internists feel that a joint is too important to be treated by surgery. To gild this lily, though too busy for ethical hanky panky, they still rate among the big five malpractitioners.

Jock Heaven

So even in neanderthaliá, an All-American defensive tackle doesn't have to sacrifice his body to pro football to make it big. There is a special niche set aside for him in medicine—orthopedics. If they can manage it through high school with a C average, have a scientific knack with saw and pliers, and the broad back of a longshoreman, they've got it made. With a little polish, the proper tailor, and keeping his mouth shut on every subject outside of bones and joints, he can— and has—clambered to the top of the golden mountain.

15

The Lord High Executioner

(Neurosurgeons)

Until recently the brain surgeon might just as well have operated with a guillotine for all the good he did. But not anymore. With new improved techniques and surgical aides such as hypothermia and cortisone, it's now known that patients are getting to the recovery room more frequently and a few lucky ones even make it to the intensive-care unit. This has greatly buoyed the neurosurgeon's ever flagging spirits.

Nonetheless the overall picture gives him no cause for real hope. It'll be a great day when he can come down from the OR like the proctologist and routinely announce, "Her hemorrhoids are out and everything is clean as a whistle," and take his bows. The neurosurgeon, who in a good week buries more than he saves, is more likely to be caught sneaking out the service elevator.

Behind a suave mask of urbanity he tries to hide his true (blue) feeling but he hasn't the control he thinks he has. When the brain surgeon's guard is down, he can be spotted halfway down the hospital corridor, looking like Li'l Abner's Joe Bflktrz, with that heavy gray pall hanging low over his head.

It's always been an enigma why men from good families with all the advantages and potential for happiness plus the usual youthful idealism about healing the sick should choose a specialty in which they attend more funerals than bar mitzvahs. Their results follow them even beyond the grave as the death rattle comes back to haunt them when they're extracting their well earned fees from executors and estates.

He is usually a cool, immaculately tailored but rather bloodless fellow whose facial expressions hide everything but the doubts that constantly nag him. He is compulsively meticulous and controlled, as he must be working arms akimbo in a hole never over an inch or two square and sometimes four inches deep. In his best cases, a deviation of only a millimeter guarantees paralysis at best, a human cauliflower at worst. It's not what one would call a rewarding specialty and if there were any self-respecting patron that would have taken on this loser it could only have been St. Jude, "dedicated to all hopeless causes."

The Virtuous Robot

The neurosurgeon leads a spartan life (with some allowable binges), otherwise he would spend more time in court than the average psychiatrist. He trains like a combination of Muhammed Ali and a Tibetan monk—in bed by ten, no sex the night before, and alcohol held down to a fifth a night guaranteeing him eight hours of sleep with a minimum of nightmares. If his ascetic life proves anything, it's that virtue has little to do with success.

He is punctilious in his personal habits and could dress just as easily in total darkness with tie, shirt, shoes, and suit matching. Everything in or out of the operating room or office is in its right place, orderly and polished, which allows him to live and work like a decerebrate cat—by well trained reflexes. Move one instrument a half-inch to the side or hang his toothbrush upside down and it'll not only precipitate a towering rage he'll remember it for a lifetime.

Though his professional record couldn't be regarded

as successful he is one of the best paid specialists and thus socially acceptable in the highest circles. Well respected and even admired among his peers, he is a hail fellow well met at the club bar and, in contrast to his losing record on patients, has a strong will to win and will probably shoot in the low eighties. He is a loner, a masochist, and an egomaniac to put the general surgeon to shame and his wife on Valium (if they haven't long since split). He is conservative in dress (wearing both suspenders and belt) and also in politics (hoping for Wallace, voting for Nixon, but preferring Reagan).

Skul-mushery

It's a behavioral puzzle why this otherwise normal-appearing man would want to spend his life dabbling in a one-and-a-half-pound mass of puddinglike substance which at best hardly does the work it's supposed to (thinking) and at worst affects every other bodily organ. Unlike the lung or kidney, which admit defeat when done for, this mushy organ gives in only grudgingly and when it does, it takes the whole body with it.

It also has one other unendearing trait. It hides behind a thick bony encasement about as impenetrable as the vaults of the Chase Manhattan. Who wouldn't give this Don Quixote of the medical profession an A for effort? He *voluntarily* works with the ills of this custardly tissue, so difficult to diagnose and almost impossible to entirely cure.

The psych, who in an even more dangerous way dabbles in the same fragile organ, looks down on the neurosurgeon as a crude workingman dealing with *his* organ in the wrong way. Psychs see him in the image of his predecessors, the medieval trephiners, who bored holes in the skull to let out the evil spirits. But the brain surgeon is hardly that crude. In fact as he goes about his diagnostic business sticking pins in the skin, banging his rubber hammer in odd places, and testing for taste and smell to see if the wires are shorted or the circuits intact, he seems more like an electrician (as farfetched as it may seem, at hourly rates a hundred times the union scale).

In the neurosurgical vale of tears, these all-time losers are now allowed at least a pittance of success. There are new procedures for controlling the bleeding in brain hemorrhages or strokes or for putting cut nerves back together again. The famous Dr. Penfield has even come up with another non-lethal operation for the neurosurgeon's peace of mind—treating the convulsing epileptic with something more than a wooden bit between the teeth. Even so, few of these sanity-saving operations give him a patient able to walk and think at the same time but it's an improvement—they're alive.

The Dandy Disc—a Best Seller

One of the more popular of these change-of-pace operations which adds to their worldly wealth as well as their batting average is one which they pioneered and publicized. In fact, the "slipped disc" is fast becoming a household word (and the best friend the tired husband ever had). From the beginning, the neurosurgeons had squatter's rights on this controversial ailment. They worked with it when no other surgeon would touch it with a ten-foot forceps and what's more they've made it into a best seller.

The venerated neuro Harvey Cushing took note of it and pioneer neurosurgeon Goldwaithe reported on a case or two. But it took a real merchandiser, Dr. Walter Dandy of Johns Hopkins, to put it across and make it pay. When this eminent prima donna stumbled on this gold mine, he brought a ray of hope to a moribund specialty. It was a shot in the arm for a trade that was then spoken of in hushed terms like syphilis.

As grasping, irascible, and biased a genius as ever set foot in an operating room, Dr. Dandy sold the procedure as a final solution to the backache problem. He evangelized in the classrooms, the garden clubs, and from the dais of medical conventions. After his first hundred cases, he wouldn't be caught asleep in church without his rubber hammer. Any patient with a back- or leg-ache who crossed his path with a knee jerk that wasn't just right (whether from a football charley horse or the third stage of syphilis) would be on the operating table at the crack of dawn and thenceforth discless, if not limp-less.

Who Cuts What on Whom

The orthopedic surgeon, who usually feels that anything bony, especially backs, is in his eminent domain, tried for a while to get in on the disc act. But his record of thousands of patients with paralysis, pain, and numbness caused by his crudeness with nerves more than offsets a generation of sagging backs produced by the bone ignorant brain surgeon. After a dozen years of open warfare there was a meeting of the minds. A treaty was hammered out, if not still altogether observed. From thenceforth the neuro would do the discs and the ortho would do the fusions, frequently in a neat little tandem whereby neither lost a cent.

Now that this is more or less settled, another battle is looming as to who does the surgery on the blood vessels (the carotids) leading to the brain and even in the brain itself. As a credibility ploy the neuros are bringing their microscopes to the OR to peer through their keyhole-size opening and connect up diseased vessels. The vasculars say that the blood vessels in the brain are too important for neurosurgeons to play around with. It is probable that this internecine dispute will be amicably settled; but knowing the egomaniacal nature of both specialties, much cerebral tissue will be spilled before they compromise somewhere between the neck and the scalp.

Mood Indigo—the Burned Brain Blues

Luckily the psychiatrists haven't made their move yet in what they consider their hemispheres of influence. But if history is to repeat itself, it won't be long. Heretofore the psychs have given the neurosurgeon only those cases which chase the sixty-five-year-old office nurse down the hall or defecate outside the office door. Until recently the lobotomy was an exercise in tranquility, mainly for the benefit of the psych. Of course the patient could then be led around on a leash, saving a lot of smashed bric-a-brac in the office. These cases he doesn't want back; with the costs of breakage figured in, he never made a cent on them anyway.

But now that there is more progress in psychosurgery, or "mood surgery" as it's called, the psych is showing more than a passing interest. Research physicians of the Dr. Strangelove ilk have found the locations in the brain that control anger, depression, or even violence (and these regions [the amygdala] deep in the recesses can only be got at with a brace and bit, the neuro's tools). By plugging in a few electrodes, these anti-social emotions can be stimulated by remote-controlled microwaves or can be abolished by scarring the area with a little current. Experimentally, they can make the hound of the Baskervilles lie side by side with the Cheshire cat or stimulate a poodle to take issue with a Doberman.

The psych has always considered any emotion his territory. Having seen his business shrunk by a two-bit tranquilizing pill, he isn't going to let anything with that cash potential float into the hands of the neurosurgeon; at least not when he sees the cases first. He also knows, like George Lincoln Rockwell, that the abundance of anger and aggression in people will make it a sure-fire consumer item and the dandiest gimmick since the id.

But as long as it's in the experimental stages and institutions such as Mass. General still get complications like blindness, loss of memory, impotency, and schizophrenia, the psychs want no part of it. They have enough troubles proving that suicides and murders aren't their fault. Still when the time is ripe, the psych will be trephining with the best of them.

But the neurosurgeon sees this threat in its proper light. Why should he worry about a competitor who can't even keep his cool just listening in the quiet of a softly lighted and soothingly decorated office? What would a psych do in the hurly-burly of the operating room with blood and tissue flying in every direction? The psych will more likely be the patient than the doctor.

As with epilepsy, stroke, or tumor of the brain, just about everything is depressing in this specialty. There's something wrong if everything turns out right. It's hard to understand the depth of masochism these M.D.s must have to put themselves through such misery. The human wreckage that emerges from the other end of this meat grinder is exactly what would be expected. Neither a general surgeon in a carload nor the most exacting plasto in Hollywood is as introverted, compulsive, and subject to depression as this high-wire doctor.

But that's not all. Like Abou Ben Adhem they lead

all the rest in malpractice and usually come out on the short end of the million-dollar suit.

The life of the neurosurgeon (both personal and professional) has few pluses. But as one involved in the scalpel art at least one accusation will never be levelled at them—unnecessary surgery (discs excluded, of course). They may be masochistic but only the worst candidate for self-lobotomy would think of going through everything a brain operation involves just for money. They may go in and find nothing, but if they do, it's an honest mistake and is probably one of the few good things that ever happen to them.

16

Yatros, Yahoos, and Yatroos:
Out of the Frying Pan
(Iatrogenesis—Doctor-caused Disease)

Most doctors are neither deliberate Yatros (those who produce disease) nor Yahoos (an endearing term Mencken applied to those who wouldn't know a disease if they got it.) But there is a combination of both of these we call Yatroos. With the techniques and drugs now at hand, statistics show that all three of these doctor types are abroad in the land. With no malice at all, they are a lethal combination.

In the past fifty years the doctor has played second fiddle to the virus, the bacillus, and the parasite. But from all reports he'll soon be number one. He's now been implicated in producing more infection, crippling, and suffering than all of the accidents caused by the internal combustion engine plus every illness foisted on the laborer by big industry from Black Lung to radium poisoning. Until now mankind has withstood the ravages of even present-day medicine, but never underestimate its power to exterminate.

For years anthropologists have pondered the disappearance of man's earliest ancestors to the Neanderthal (one of his last). It's no longer a secret—it must have been the doctor. There is now concrete evidence brought forth by Dr. Guido Majno in his book *Man and Wound in the Ancient World* that early man had come up against a primeval doctor—and, as usual, lost.

We know that early man's skull was drilled and his bones were set. What we don't know is what drugs were used on him, how much he was experimented with, or if there was an AMA. If all of these conditions were present, it would have hastened extinction considerably. If our ape-man progenitors, who had phenomenal strength and staying power, could live in freezing caves, searing tundras, or steaming jungles but could not survive the primitive doctor—what chance have we? Puny and protected, overfed and overheated, it seems we're in for it.

Fragile as it may appear, human protoplasm, which has withstood pollution and inflation and the biggest maimer of them all, the automobile, is no set-up. But on the other hand, neither is the medical profession.

Them Against Us

So it won't be a pushover. Humanity has so far held the doctors at bay by producing two for one. Overpopulation has saved the day—but not for long. Who's in the forefront of the whole movement for population control with International Planned Parenthood and Zero Population? The doctors, of course. If it weren't for some of those technical slip-ups (8 percent of the pills and 3 percent of the IUDs are defective) it would be curtains in a matter of decades. Although these loopholes give hope, this must be balanced against medical *progress* with drugs that create disease, crippling surgical procedures, lobotomies, chemotherapy, and X rays that promote cancer. This is not to mention nuclear medicine which is only in its infancy and may well do the whole trick all by itself.

Consider for instance the diabolical scheme to expose and deliver most patients into the hands of doctors —hospital insurance. It's a siren song few patients can resist. Imagine getting bed and board and even relief from ills and family problems for a mere pittance. Once snared, anything can happen and usually does. This hospital thing is no mere bagatelle. As starters, we have over a million-and-a-half infections (usually staff) acquired in these institutions each year. In an experiment in Boston, even with a new antibiotic to combat it, 40 percent of those infected died. But the cleverness of it all! Who carries these deadly germs? You guessed it—doctors, nurses, and interns. Patients will have to go some to beat these ploys. Not long ago chloroform killed or maimed 50 percent of those who inhaled it for surgery. With nerve chemicals and anesthetics like Halothane, only the innate strength of the human held this mortality down to 35,000 to 40,000 last year. This is not counting complications such as brain damage, blindness, paralysis, and liver failure. Blood transfusions did in around 5,000 and there were 100,000 cases of hepatitis. Wrong medication creates a whopping 100 million cases a year—and so it goes.

Killing With Kindness

If this were a simple open-and-shut case of malice aforethought, where a patient could defend himself and the doctor stand accused, it would be one thing. But it's not. It's much more insidious. Not only do most physicians practice with no evil intent, but they do it with all the altruism and compassion they have time for. This isn't much to brag about but at least it's not purposeful homicide, which is commendable. We all understand and commiserate with human error, though it's small consolation to the loved one having dirt shoveled on his casket.

In all candor, the profession, with honorable intent,

maims tenfold the number of patients injured either by negligence or malpractice. But is it the doctor's fault when he gives a patient MER 29 to lower cholesterol (by the same wonderful people that gave us thalidomide) and it causes cataracts? Was it not on the best advice of a detail man who has a college education with an A.B. degree in Urban Studies? If you can't trust a multibillion-dollar industry like pharmaceutical firms, whom can you trust? Could the M.D. even begin to study the literature on the thousands of new drugs on the market each year, even if the experiments were on the up-and-up and the researchers didn't tamper with their results?

The Food and Drug Administration spends half its time checking the hanky-panky of experimenters who'll change a figure or two to look good enough for that headline "Cancer Cure in Sight," or "Common Cold Finished?" But in our democracy a little shading never hurt. Doesn't the Labor Department minimize the unemployment figures and doesn't the Department of Agriculture hide a Russian wheat deal? So penicillin makes some two million patients a year sicker than they were. Isn't it to the profession's credit that only a few thousand of those die? The thalidomide side effects on rats slipped a researcher's mind—but would it necessarily have the same effect on babies? Some of these results may be purposefully hidden, but generally the drug companies have the patient's interest at heart—if it doesn't interfere too much with profits.

How should a surgeon know after forty years of using sterilized talc on his gloves that it was the cause of a million iron-bound adhesions, tying up the bowels so tight it would take two more operations to unravel them? He may be only trying to help, but killing with kindness is tough to stave off. If an escaped convict is coming at you with a gun and knife, you can at least try to protect yourself or run. On the other hand, one doesn't visit the Manson family ranch in California for that rundown feeling. When a kindly doctor comes, offering health and happiness, who looks that gift horse in the mouth?

Who Chases What?

Although ambulance chasing by doctors has grown into a nice little sideline, they really don't need it. It's the patient, sick or not, that seeks them out and hunts them down, practically begging to have his body and his mind exposed, manipulated, and injected. Any doctor will do. Few patients have an inkling of the intelligence or the ability of the doctor they go to, any more than they know their auto mechanic's. And once they're there, it's the rare one who questions what the doctor prescribes or injects, much less what he has. They'll take any pill, subject themselves to every physical indignity, and allow every surgical insult with hardly a query (even if they question, who answers?).

Help Stamp Out Health

As doctors say, every capsule, every injection, every operation is a calculated risk. Yet it's been shown from studies at Yale and Cornell that by the consummate skill of the physician alone illness caused by prescribed drugs is kept down to only 1,400,000 hospitalizations a year. But the record in the hospitals is much more impressive. With a more scientific approach by the best of American medicine (including medical school-affiliated hospitals and their professors and the most up-to-date scientific apparatus), they caused only 5 million diseases—and true dedication managed to save all but 200,000 of them. This is a record that Chrysler and GM couldn't equal with their recall of defective cars. This salvaging of almost 4,800,000 patients from the diseases doctors themselves produce is remarkable.

Judgments must be made, but can he be on the lookout every minute, every day, for that case where penicillin (which cures gonorrhea) causes instant death from allergic shock? Or for that one arthritis case a month which comes down with diabetes, psychosis, high blood pressure, bleeding ulcers, and cataracts from cortisone? Would he be human if he were on constant alert for every local anesthesia, tranquilizer, anticoagulant, liver biopsy, cardiac catheterization, and a hundred other miracle drugs and surgical procedures which can maim and blind? He would hardly have time to make a living, never mind his Wednesdays, weekends, and nights off. But if this is the best—what about the worst?

"I'm No Crook"

According to the AMA, there *are* no worst. Neither among the rank and file nor within those ivy walls will they admit of one Yatro or a Yahoo. As to a Yatroo, perish the thought. They unequivocally reject the idea that an ignoramus or a fraud could actually graduate medical school, even though recently physicians have taken more than their fair share of front-page news as murderers, pushers, and tax evaders. The AMA attitude is understandable. Every union is out to protect its dues payers, even if they include 3,600 dope addicts and 5,000 alcoholics among them. The New York State quarterly report listed not a single case of abuse or fraud in medical services, while the U.S. attorney was preparing cases against nine clinics and 109 doctors for fraudulent practices. Even patients won't believe their doctor has fraudulent or quackish tendencies until he suddenly disappears from practicing in the outside world.

When one gets right down to it, it's the doctor's character that patients have faith in. They know in their hearts that if a state senator, a congressman, or the chairman of the board of ITT recommends a student and he is admitted to Med school, he must be a fine young man of sound moral fiber, even if he got caught buying his thesis.

But the final Good Housekeeping seal of approval is stamped on by the caliber of the internship and residency a young doctor gets. And once in training it's up to the professional fraternity to keep a patient's confidence high by hiding a young surgeon's incompetence, the schizoid tendencies in a young psych, or a budding pederast's interest in proctology.

So there may be an outside chance that an occasional Yatro or Yahoo may slip through the screening process. Even at the summit, the brilliant young researcher of the Sloan-Kettering Research staff, who admitted he falsified his research reports on a promising new cancer approach, may be treating your best friend for leukemia. Your wife, unsuspecting (at first), may be in the hands (hands-hmmm!) of the psychofornicist Dr. Hartogs twice weekly; or your daughter visiting one of those golden-gloved hysterectomizers. This is not to mention your grandmother, unsafe and unsound in one of Mr. Bergman's doctor-supervised New York nursing homes.

Some of My Best Friends Are Yatroos

There are Yatroos everywhere, securely imbedded in that layer of middle America, AMA dues payers who do every patient they can. They've padded Medicare with tests and visits to the point of bankruptcy and have Medicaid (for the poorest) on its knees with their clinics and Park Avenue fees. They take a thousand X rays without film, give ten thousand injections with sterile water, and have well patients coming back forever for fictitious diseases. All of these public servants, plus the diet doctor, the pill doctor, and the ones who do a quarter of a million dollars a year in vitamin injections also passed their state boards, have specialty diplomas, privileges at the best hospitals, and are officers in the best associations, academies, and specialty boards of examiners.

These are the respectable Yatroos who quietly but consciously do what they do. Then there are others who are more to be pitied than censured—and should themselves be under treatment. One in every forty young M.D. graduates will become a dope addict and pusher; an even larger number will have to have two Gibsons before breakfast to steady their hands on the neck of a tough thyroid case. A considerable proportion of those 25,000 psychiatrists have schizoid symptoms which make a wall-climbing psychotic out of a simple neurotic. And then there is that poor old senile family physician who constantly gets mixed up giving digitalis to the hemorrhoid case and sending the failing heart to be anoscoped.

What They Don't Know Could Hurt Them

Though the profession may have its share of individual dupes, dopes, and criminals, the system itself isn't lily white. The cold fact is that whether a patient would ever think so or not, his doctor does experiment on him. How can a researcher be sure that that pill that cured a rat of diabetes doesn't cause coronaries in a human (as it does) unless it's tried on one? Who did they do the first open heart surgery on—a poltergeist? How many arthritics did they try cortisone on before they found them bleeding from ulcers? It's not really hush-hush like the C.I.A. and its L.S.D. experiments, for though the fact is not advertised, there is nothing new about human guinea pigs. Anyway, with the AMA ethics committee and the FDA as watchdogs, why worry?

At their worst, however scientifically bent, the American doctor would never do it with such gusto as the Nazis did. It's one thing testing a new sleeping pill on insomniacs and another infecting Poles with tetanus or freezing Jews in ice water. We are now much more civilized and since the civil rights law of 1964 it's illegal to fool around with ethics. No more of those Alabama syphilis experiments on the blacks by the Public Health Service (health service??). That's out. Most of the experimental work in the United States is now done on those patients either uncomprehending or of little value like the retarded, senile patients in veteran hospitals, prisoners with little choice, those in mental institutions, or children. By carefully picking and choosing we've come up with cardiac catheterization, new daring operations, and hundreds of wonder drugs with just a little gamble. Even in the case of the thirty infants in New York who had their spines tapped —the parents never knew and no one was the worse for it.

In medicine's more altruistic and humane times, doctors used to experiment on themselves first. But that was before the efficiency and economy experts showed what a waste it was, when ordinary patients come so cheap and easy.

The $200-a-day Guinea Pig

There's one other item on the iatrogenic scorecard which may be hazardous to a patient's health. It's the doctor's dilemma in training the young physicians. For instance, if well trained board-certified specialists from the best institutions can produce such a plethora of disease and complications, think what trouble a first-year intern in a rural or ghetto hospital can cause. It wasn't so bad years ago when the poor and indigent patients were on free wards for the very purpose of training the neophite. Now there is no such thing as a free patient. But as with experimentation, no private patient would think his doctor would let a young intern practice on him. Yet with practically everyone insured, residents must either operate on private patients or on each other. And guess who?

It's Better to Have Coped and Lost...

So there is our hero stripped to the buff without his make up or put on. Not exactly all Oslers, Menningers, or Cooleys but not all Bonnies and Clydes either. An unfortunately small percent of them are intelligent, dedicated, hard-working, compassionate, and moral and this is no small achievement. But the big question is, can the patient eventually win out over the ravages of the Yatros, Yahoos, and Yatroos? Can mother nature cope, or will we be the next Neanderthal disappearing act, done in by our own healers?

Our medical opponent is not unworthy. He is neither haphazard in his approach nor lacking skill and persistence. He will use every instrument and technique at his command and invent new ones if necessary. He will forever seek out all avenues in the pursuit of science using not only the body but the mind, not only the sick but the well, not the aged alone but also the young and the strong. Nor is time of the essence in his onward rush to cure. And if debilitation and destruction must follow them all the days of their lives:

> Ashes to ashes, and dust to dust,
> If science doesn't get you, medicine must.

17

The Deadly Game:
Hot Cross Bones
(Pathology, Chemotherapy)

There are two very specialized specialists—the path-ologist and the chemotherapist as examples of a group —who in all fairness to the patient should have emblazoned over their office doors, "Beware all ye who enter here." For most who do enter, it's a one-way crossing of the River Styx. Black crepe bows should be permanently affixed to the entrance to ac-centuate the negative. These two would look more natural over a steaming cauldron than over a micro-scope. When the pathologist is at it, the patient by any other name is called cadaver, and it's later than you think when the chemotherapist begins his trial by nausea.

Though these macabre losers must be riddled with a mélange of psychological complexes, they seem to thrive on their work. In the old werewolf days these unholy two would have succumbed only when a splinter from the original cross was driven through their hearts.

The Crown Prince of Darkness

The first of them, the chemotherapist, looks every bit the refugee from a chemistry lab. He is artless and guileless, and does his job as if he's working on any

168

other chemical compound fizzing in a test tube; only this particular one happens to eat and breathe.

This M.D. with his chemically stained personality is given a fishy eye by the more respected members of the medical community. It's as if he were part of the inorganic world, some sort of inert element not yet refined. His appearance in his laboratory coat of many colors with sleeves hanging below the dye-smudged fingers, does little to enhance his almost preternatural presence. His tattle-tale gray pallor is probably the result of inhaling lung-consuming fumes from the concoctions he cooks up. What this does to his brain is anyone's guess, but judging from his behavior, it's not good.

Chemotherapists neither look nor act like physicians, even though their lives are dedicated to righting the bodily scourges. They are more like chemists involved in disease than doctors using chemistry. From their earliest histories, they were the kids who blew up the high school chemistry lab and, when more "mature," were the ones who conjured up compounds that would make the H-bomb scientist, Edward Teller, cringe. Their latter-day delight is in observing gobs of luridhued combinations wipe out colonies of microbes or tissue cells on a petri dish, even if perchance they later eliminate the rats, dogs, chimps, and anything else they touch.

Cadavers Are Forever

It's known that patients injected with some of their solutions have passed to their reward so thoroughly perfused that they save the price of embalming and could probably be set up in a public park, unbronzed, withstanding the elements longer and better than General Grant's horse. The crematoriums even find it necessary to add an extra charge for the disposition of these final remains, as some corpses won't ignite at even 5,000 degrees Fahrenheit. Families who get the urn with the remains have been known to reject them complaining that their grandmother could not have been reduced to a malachite green cinder that glows with an eerie fluorescence.

These chem docs may have some little rapport with pathologists and maybe even a working relationship with oncologists (cancer specialists), but rarely with patients or patients' families. Families have even been known to complain that some of these doctors not only look and act but smell like death. This is an accusation they resent. Though the compounds they work with usually give off a stench of exhumed stevedores, they can't help its clinging qualities. They knowingly accept this stigma in the interest of science—and their intense curiosity as to how far they can go mixing chemicals and humans.

Where Is Thy Sting

But it's not only their odor or the sensitivity of the patient's family. Other doctors and nurses seem to hold them at arm's length with the rightful suspicion that if the chemotherapist is called can St. Peter be far behind? But even more they resent their lack of graciousness. Most doctors have some respect for death, and it's always considered a nice sort of amenity to allow a certain peace and comfort in those final minutes. But all the way to the death rattle the chemo pushes stuff with all sorts of radium-tagged elements and toxic World War I gases that can make a patient sicker, more nauseated, more weakened, and more ready and willing to be taken.

Other than making the already afflicted patient

deathly ill, the other big drawback to chemotherapy has not yet been completely worked out. Those fizzing, bubbling compounds unquestionably eat through cancers, lymph nodes, and blood vessels clogged with wild-growing white cells with no trouble at all. The kicker is that by the same token they can also eat through a trencherman's boot. These imaginative compounds are not very discreet. As they destroy tumors or diseases in the liver, spleen, or kidney, they have a knack of taking the good with the bad—which can be most unhealthy. In Slabsville this is known as dissolving the baby in the bath water.

These bespotted souls shouldn't be blamed for all the patients' problems. After all, chemotherapy is only in its infancy. If they can't solve all of the problems in the laboratory using man's closest ancestor, the chimpanzee, they just have to bring the laboratory to the bedside. That's where the trouble lies.

Sure it may be a shot (if a parting shot) in the dark now. But who knows, someday it may cure something. Sir Alexander Fleming was supposedly looking for a cancer cure when he found penicillin. Maybe someone looking for a new miracle drug for impotence will accidentally (it's usually accidental) hit on a cancer cure that won't kill. So with this in mind, it still deserves the good old college try. Either way it won't be a total loss. It's been found that many of the compounds are useful for clearing barnacles off of ship bottoms.

Slabsville

The pathologist, Mr. Effeat, is the professional next of kin to the chemo. This brother under the skin is made of sterner stuff than most physicians. He's 100 percent science with no art at all—after all, how much can a bedside manner do with a corpse? This glinty-eyed one is mentioned only in hushed tones for the simple reason that the finality of his words can strike terror into the family doctor who prescribed the *final* medication, the surgeon who left the clamp in, or the nurse who forgot to refill the oxygen tank. No matter how much others try to delude or escape the morbid facts, Mr. Truth and Consequences brings them painfully back to terra firma. To him, the dead man tells the tale. He's got the goods on all who sin and it's rarely good goods. He seldom, if ever, misdiagnoses for it's all down in red, blue, and green on little glass slides.

He's a peculiar type for a doctor—he wouldn't know a live breathing patient if one jumped off the slab. Life is prologue, death is the only life worth knowing. His own life is spent in the quiet cool of the morgue where he does his postmortems, taking everything out, putting nothing back in, telling where it all went wrong and sending back the verdict, which usually makes few doctors happy and few lawyers unhappy. The only people he delights in are going, going, or gone, and if they're interesting enough, he is wont to wait for them. If he can't get the whole, he'll settle for some of their parts.

Paradoxically, he's paid better for dealing with mortified flesh and blood than most of his colleagues are for aiding life itself. (One such in Maryland is quoted at over $450,000 for the year.) And for good reason, for with the surge in hospital business, new anesthesia, and iatrogenics (diseases created by doctors themselves) there'll soon be need for more pathologists than dermatologists or even plastic surgeons.

The Excretomancers

Everything that this anthropophagic gnome touches, from the stiff to the glass slide, is cold and inanimate.

If he has feelings at all, they're manifested only in the fix of his vulturous eye when successfully conning a corpse from a bereaved family. Pathologists carry on their necromancy hidden away in the bowels of the hospital but do it with the same gusto they once showed toying with the innards of a frog in Biology I.

Other than the routine biopsy, the pathologists' only link with the patient, the ill, or just the living is through bodily waste. They are the keepers of the lab. In this sideline, they show almost a childish delight in the color, odor, consistency, and composition of the detritis eliminated from any ailing bodily orifice or tissue. Today, since most of this is done by computerized instruments, they don't even have the pleasure and challenge of matching their senses against a particularly puzzling specimen of excrement. But whatever they do, even the dead things in life aren't free. In this three-billion-dollar-a-year business they charge for every drop of blood, every spritz of urine, every shred of tissue routinely sent through their processes. As with the surgeons and diet doctors, it's cash on the barrel head—even to macreate a stiff.

These specialists of the macabre have one particular subspecialty that dotes not only on death but on violent death, showing no interest in the run-of-the-mill deceased or diseased who die with their boots off. Once called coroners, these medical examiners are the least introverted of this breed as they must spend some time in court, which means at least minimal contact with the living. In this role, it may be their word on which will hang a prisoner or a millon-dollar malpractice suit. They have a special attraction to murders—especially political ones. D. Milton Helpern, formerly of New York's ghoul squad with 35,000 cases to handle in one year, was kept so busy figuring out where the bullets went in, came out, and who and how many pulled the trigger, he had no time for the poisonings, bombings, suicides, and other less exciting cases. Helpern in his day has saved more souls than a South Side Chicago priest and created more lifers than Tom Dewey at his best.

Humane? Human? Humus!

The chemo and patho are only two of a kind. In a gentler way there are a host of other fellow travelers of this ilk. None are exactly examples of professional life to hold up to an idealistic medical student impatient to eliminate the suffering of humankind, rather than humankind itself.

It can't be said that many or any of these specialists of the end game don't have some kind of genetic warp or at least a conditioned woof. How could an ordinary human (or professional for that matter) enjoy that last affair, their sole function presiding over the dissolution of the human corpus? Even though they may ask themselves where they went wrong, it's problematic whether any of them would change it if they could. Yet no mother brought her son into the world to wind up as assistant resident to the Grim Reaper.

18

The Blue Cross Hilton Uptown:
Hospital Heal Thyself

One hopeful sign that man will survive a nuclear holocaust is that he has sometimes managed to survive the hospitals. Any patient that can fend off the hordes of hospital staph, make it through an anesthetic with no brain damage, avoid a mismatched transfusion, then overcome the more routine misdiagnosis and medication errors, and still not come out feet first is hardier than the proverbial cockroach.

Hospitals are fine if you're not sick. Barring the food and the noise, it's as good a place to rest and relax as the Caribe Hilton. But if you need diagnosis, treatment, and gentle care, that's something else again. The modern hospital is no place for maudlin sentimentality. Once and for all one must realize that those steel-and-glass mastodons of architecture are no longer missions of mercy just catering to the ill, but branch offices of the federal and private insurance industry. When they were run by Sisters of Mercy and manna from heaven, it was one thing. Today, administered by masters of efficiency and cold Blue Cross-Medicare-Medicaid cash, it's another.

It's not that comptrollers, accountants, and cost experts lack heart, but like today's string beans or lamb chops, sickness must be carefully weighed, packaged, and paid for, with a little profit for the house. Everything in the hospital from an aspirin to a gargle has a price —except perhaps politeness or compassion, which are unavailable at any price.

Give Me Your Bored, Your Puccied, Your Guccied

Disease, patient care, doctors, and nurses are supposedly their business, but other facets of the hospital are just as crucial. There is more to it than just healing. First and foremost it must be pleasant and comfortable for visitors, doctors, cost accountants, technicians, and the gray ladies. It must also be a thing of beauty so that every director of the board can proudly point to a wing and say, "I gave that."

Is it not unique for any institution other than Schrafft's or Bergdorf's to say give us your jaded, your bored, your Puccied and Guccied housewife one day a week as a respite from shopping and *As the World Turns* to play Florence Nightingale without a tinge of vomitus spotting her starched and chevroned uniform?

What better training ground for our young Ben Caseys than an internship to launch them into the world of stockbrokers, country clubs, and the tax bite, while learning the more mundane task of conquering disease? Where better to learn the ways of striking for more wages and less work, or practicing the art of squeezing the last drop out of an insurance policy?

Sugar Daddy, Blue

Blue Cross is the best thing that has happened to hospitals (and doctors) since tonsillectomy and Congress' Hill-Burton Bill (which opened Fort Knox to put up those houses that Uncle's Jack built). Blue Cross and Medicare, which the AMA fought against as the entering wedge of socialized medicine, is the principal means of support of both doctor and hospitals. Without it only Getty, Muhammad Ali, or a Catfish

Hunter could afford the one hundred to two hundred dollars a day cover charge. And now that insurance pays for everything from Kleenex to throwaway X ray machines, the Shah couldn't do it with more opulence.

No matter how you slice it, the Big Blue coverage and the efficiency expert's thousand ways of milking it made the hospital look as if it was born to the purple. Those geniuses showed in black and white that an enema wasn't something to be flushed away; it's an economic package of soap, water, paper, hourly wage, and depreciation that Blue Cross must pay $1.76 for. But that's just the beginning: Everything a patient imbibes, ingests, or is exposed to has a price, which of course is over and above the overnight charge.

A pair of aspirins costs Blue Cross what a drugstore charges for a bottle. It's $350 as the cart is wheeled across the OR threshold and another $150 as soon as the mask is clapped over the nose (with anethetists' fees besides). An average hospital's lab, X ray, and pharmacy would be a safer, and more lucrative investment than A.T. and T. bonds; some knock down a cool ten to fifteen million a year.

But it's all in the Big Blue game hospitals play, as brick and mortar, decorator colors and marble floors, board rooms and lounges must all be depreciated. Blue pays for full-time chiefs, teaching, and even publicity at Tiffany prices. But the beauty of it all is that it's not a lot of skin off anyone's individual nose. Sure the patient pays in the end but even the ten-year 175 percent increase in premiums comes in dribs and drabs, which is almost painless.

With all of that cash flowing in you'd think their books would be as black as the Chase Manhattan's. But not hospitals; their balances sag like a face lift in its fifth year. They've learned to live so high on the hog it would strike awe and respect in the hearts of those deficit barons of Penn Central. This red ink phenomenon is as certain and universal as its inedible food, and, like the poor, it'll always be with them. No matter the endowment windfall, the subtle gouging, or the city, state, and federal funds that pour in, at fiscal time its cupboard is as bare as old Mother Hubbard's.

It is even more of an enigma, considering another hospital phenomenon. As soon as big business, such as the American Hospital Corporation, gets in on the healing game, buying up hundreds of private hospitals (owned mostly by doctors), red ink turns to black overnight.

The Good Samaritan and the I.R.S.

Any other business run like the average voluntary hospital would have gone the way of the corner grocery or the honest mechanic, but, as a heaven-sent institution of mercy, hospitals have their guardian angels. Where else can those generous angels, the new conglomerate manipulations and the international junk dealers, buy instant respectability, ten times their money's worth in publicity, and a seat at the right hand of St. Peter at Internal Revenue's expense? And if it costs a million or two, his name chiseled over a clinic is a better long-term investment than the Triborough Bridge. The Sinatra wing in Palm Springs helped redeem an image tarnished by booze, broads, and baccarat.

Most of these big-hearted mercy healers of the multinational corporation type found this new mission in life (giving instead of taking) via their personal physician. In turn that lucky M.D. who managed to hustle a real live turkey onto a board doesn't suffer either. Regardless of whether he can differentiate migraine from hangover, after the first six-figure check clears, this healer is headed for hospital stardom.

The Vice President in Charge of Deficits

Before hospitals were big business, they used to be administered by a superintendent, either a nurse whose bunions had got the best of her or a retired engineer who could patch up the steam boiler on weekends and still keep his own bank balance straight. In that antiquated if solvent system the deficits weren't so large but neither had Blue Cross and Parkinson's law found each other. Also at that time the ladies' auxiliaries and the patients' arts and crafts department didn't have priority over the nursing department. In those days the administrator took orders from one of the chiefs, usually the head surgeon.

It's all changed now that superintendents are for school buildings and the city water works. Nothing but an M.D. director is good enough for the modern board of directors—how can one pull in NIH grants with a plumber at the head? Anyway, the ladies auxiliary needs the prestige of a doctor for its annual dinner soireé. This gent is also made a vice president of the institution so he gets chosen as if the directors were choosing a high official in the oil or automobile business. He is mostly culled from the ranks of physicians who made it big in the stock market or real estate, or are dropouts from public health or government service because their wives demanded more than those crummy commissary privileges.

When the nondoctor was in charge, he was constantly reminded by the doctors that one had to have an M.D. to have "an insight into hospital problems." Today, with the annual budgets running into the hundreds of millions, the doctor director is constantly reminded by the board that he's only a doctor and doesn't know anything about high finance. Whichever he is supposed to be, who needs to spend six years training how to treat athlete's foot or watery diarrhea to deal with the ego of doctors, the hysterics of head nurses, and the high cost of throwaway needles? Who needs to learn how to identify cirrhosis of the liver so he can settle a laundry strike?

A Dillar a Dollar Who Needs a Scholar?

When one speaks of hospitals, not only does the image of Dr. Welby flash through the mind but also that young intern, Dr. Kildare. Usually the intern sought out the best hospital where he could get the best training while working practically free, night and day. With this kind of concentrated toil even the intellect of a medical graduate was able to pick up enough so he could safely be let loose on the general public. Now interns demand junior exec wages, weekends off, and vacation with pay. In the old days he was thankful for a quick catch-as-catch-can roll with a student nurse in the linen closet as his only R and R.

Today it's all changed; that once devil-may-care bachelor intern is already an old married man, with kids yet, before he knows which end of the stethoscope is up. His prime interest is what's in it for him; salary, fringe benefits, and time for moonlighting to make more. The hospital's university affiliations, its training programs, or even its accreditation are afterthoughts. For $3,000 more a year he'll go to a substandard first aid station, waiting to learn the fine points of reading an EKG or diagnosing gout until he's out and on his own. He's still dedicated, idealistic, and full of human compassion; but what does that have to do with knocking off at five sharp to go home to the family, whether he's in the middle of a physical examination or holding a retractor for a surgeon cutting deep into someone's bowel?

P.R. vs. R.I.P.

At one time, the hospital was known by the number of people it healed. It's still nice for Sloan-Kettering and Cornell Medical Center to keep beds for the ill and relieve suffering, if only to show their big donors they care. But there's not a one of them that wouldn't trade a nursery baby cured of staph infection for one Nobel laureate in the lab. As far as a hospital's image goes, a Christiaan Barnard or an Irving Cooper in the operating room is worth a hundred saved cardiac arrests in the emergency room. Whoever heard of the Groot Schuur Hospital in Capetown, South Africa (of all places), before hearts were transplanted or of St. Barnabas Hospital in the Bronx before Parkinson surgery? Has any hospital ever made the front page for the speed of its bedpan service or the aroma of its coffee? It's the hospital's image that counts. A hospital on the move doesn't spend a good slice on a J. Walter Thompson protégé to waste his talents on how many patients get their medication on time or whether they walk out alive or not.

A new 70-million-volt X ray unit that can burn through a brick wall is the stuff grants are made of. Making the news is what inclines a well heeled ninety-year-old dowager to change her will. A bath two days late or the patient awakened at 4 A.M. for his sleeping pill is forgotten once back home. It's the image that attracts flamboyant surgeons and the research doctors that get the grants that make the news that supports the house that Jack built.

And as Dr. John Knowles, once director of Mass. General, will tell you, you don't get to head the Rockefeller Foundation without being in the news. And it takes a top image-maker to get you there. They're not only handy at playing up the hospital administration but also at playing down adverse publicity about strikes, embezzlements, and malpractice suits. They're worth their weight in gold for burying the court cases near the obituaries and putting the heart transplant (if it lived one hour) in the Sunday rotogravure. This shouldn't be taken in the wrong spirit. It doesn't mean the hospital is just image conscious or that the patient doesn't count, it's only a sign of the times.

The Paper Doctors

After the P.R. offices are firmly established, the first hint that a hospital has gone big time is when the specialists are moved in and the G.P.s out. This is done quietly with the notice to the staff that "only board-qualified physicians will be admitted for privileges as of this date." Then the general doctor, who did the teaching *free* and was available for an accident case, sees the handwriting on the wall and knows the squeeze is on.

The next clue that the hospital is willing to go the way of all flesh and abandon the patient, bed bath, back rub, and all is the slow infiltration of full-time chiefs. The hospital begins by recruiting the best and the brightest who have misspent their youth in the laboratory (not on a ward), have an allergic aversion to the sick, and have published an esoteric article or two on something that has nothing to do with stuff like cure or care. They're a dime a dozen these days since most young doctors now long for the leisurely professorial life. It's also good for a hospital on the make; Blue Cross pays for these quasi-professors, and it brings a little class to those more commercial-minded specialists who clutter the institution. It's the wave of the future and getting worse. (More than one-third of all licensed doctors in the United States are administrators who specialize in paper only.)

In contrast to the old clinician who used to come into a room, sniff, and say, "It's typhoid," or look at the patient's nails and begin treating tuberculosis, this breed had all of its senses atrophied by the time it hit the hospital. With a greater array of laboratory instruments and clinical equipment at their disposal than the Houston Backup, these doctors are bent on using every one to save them from too time-consuming patients. They may eventually cause Blue Cross to be put up for public auction, but no one can say they weren't thorough. They may have difficulty differentiating a fever blister from a chancre but tropical schistosomiasis may be the diagnosis even if the patient never left Alaska.

They're well salaried and have their own hours: never on Sundays, Saturdays, lab days, teaching days, or during convention cruises or safaris.

The Physicians of Self Destruct

There's only one occupational hazard that these full-timers are heir to. They must treat and operate on each other or on each other's families as a show of respect and support. This could mean the eventual self-elimination of them all. For instance, one research surgeon at a well-known university-affiliated hospital, who handles a knife like an orangutan peeling a banana, operated on the chief of medicine for a gallbladder and severed the unfortunate professor's main duct by mistake. It could have been the end of him except for one of the "commercial doctors" who saved the day.

There's usually a high turnover in these misplaced academicians. After a few months it's seen that their administrative ability can't solve the paper-clip problem and second year medical students stump them on ward rounds. The final straw is when a board member submits to their care and there are complications.

At present many hospitals have hit on hard times. Pills that cure at home and pills that contracept have emptied contagious wards and obstetrical buildings, and pills that relax have depleted the mental hospitals. Also with the government picking up the tab, they're now looking over the hospital's shoulder to make sure the patients wouldn't be better off on a cruise or in a tennis camp. But given the hospital's resilience and powers of improvising, those steel and stone monuments will eventually come up with all the answers, placating the government and creating a full house with bigger and better deficits.

19

The Blue Cross Hilton Downtown:
The Patient's Not for Burning

In this era of laser beams, open heart surgery, and electronic monitoring, the patient and the bedpan are largely lost in the shuffle. There's nothing wrong with every hospital wanting to become the next Mayo Clinic, as long as the patient isn't left to molder between the sheets, crumbs and all.

These modern skyscrapers of T.L.C. and the healing arts were built with federal money to get the ill and the old taken care of with minimum risk of being infected, crippled, poisoned, or actually burned alive in the firetraps of the '30s. Now in the '70s, in our new high-rise towers, there are no more fires, no more roaches in the hash, no more peeling walls, and also no more patient care than the chimp gets on the research floor below. Through the compassion and good offices of our congressmen, the sick and dying were taken out of the world of shaky tinder boxes and into the brave new scientific world of full-time professors, open heart surgery, bed sores, linen rash, and the waiting game. Getting that shot, that pain pill or urinal, or the scarcest commodity in the hospital market—a nurse—is a chancy shot.

If you are deathly ill and want your body monitored by everything but a kind soul and a gentle hand, go to the professors at Bellevue or the Mayos. On the other hand, if you want your hernia fixed and a bedpan when you need it, find the smallest hospital, where your family doctor can still practice—even if the intern speaks only Sanskrit. The wrong diagnosis, the other patient's medicine, and the mismatched blood are no more likely there than at the Presbyterian in New York, but if you're thirsty you'll get a drink.

Without Race, Creed, or Logic

The large new edifice complexes admit they're not real big on service but everything else must be first class, including the doctors. Not just any licensed M.D. can come in and practice, even if he's treated you for thirty years and knows you inside and out. An internist with an extra diploma (office hours by appointment only) must be brought in, so that there's no chance of beginning treatment until every test and examination that the family doctor has done a dozen times is repeated, even if it takes a week, at $200 a day. Any hospital that wants to make it big in the American Hospital Association must first purge itself of the family physician (or anything else smacking of warmth or common sense). Licensed or not, a doctor must pass not only special boards but also ethnic, color, national, and blue-blood tests—according to each hospital's image.

Mr. Livingstone I Presume

So frequently the patient comes into a hospital where everything is strange, including his doctor, whom he's never seen before. With this kind of short-term contract many a patient can wander the corridors for days without a kind word or treatment for his high blood pressure. Weekends are bad enough, but patients have been known to be forgotten for as long as two weeks (around vacation time or Christmas). Getting lost is one thing, less lucky ones may never make it out. When dealing in masses of patients on the march to health and with the fast-food-franchise philosophy of "take-your-number—out—and next," things can go awry even in the most computerized institution.

There are special periods, in the day-in, day-out hospital routines, when it's dangerous even in the intensive care unit—monitors and all. To be admitted for a serious illness in July when the new interns come in (or before they've learned to speak English) or during strikes is just courting disaster (it's only the patient who may not survive the picket line). If a diabetic comes in on Thursday with sugar in his urine and Friday is the Fourth of July, it may be all over before the fireworks end.

The Ninety-minute Hour

But this is the kind of care for the patient who has everything. How about the poor and the indigent? What poor and indigent? They went out with the free clinic and the house call. Some kind of insurance or agency, government or otherwise, takes care of everyone. There is no such thing anymore as a free anything. A hospital in a pinch may get stuck with an uninsured emergency, but only rarely. The sign on the emergency room wall is explicit: "Show your card, plunk down your $35, or bleed elsewhere."

Since the long lost end of the old-fashioned house call, the emergency room has become the rich and poor man's general practitioner—Dr. Muhammad wouldn't go to the mountain, so the patient goes to the emergency room. These medical crossroads are like the

Kasbah on Saturday night. They are full to capacity twenty-four hours a day, operated with a dispatch that has cut waiting time from a two- to a one-meal stay. It's become not only a great meeting place but a great leveler—rich and poor waiting side by side, with the rich having less than a two-hour advantage. Once you catch the doctor's eye, if not bled-out or in shock from reception room fatigue, there are facilities to run up bills of four or five hundred dollars and with an extra half-hour and a few more tests, the annual checkup could be skipped. It's now big business—employing experienced doctors at a hefty salary just to manage the traffic.

Whither? On the Vine

So whither the hospital, whither medicine—wither the patient on the vine? The portent of things to come, the real clue that medicine in general and hospitals in particular are going to go the way of the neighborhood butcher, is the Fall of the House of Nightingale. Hospital nursing schools are just about finished, which says a lot about where the patients stand in the hearts of the medical establishment. Full-time chiefs can be underwritten, research can be subsidized, and volunteers trained to man the telephones and soda fountains, but if nursing schools can't earn their keep—out they go. It's the bottom line, not the bottom that obviously counts.

The once hard-working Cinderellas, those kindly bedpan jockeys who could create bliss with a rub of the back or the punch of a pillow, or give an enema with delicacy and compassion, have been replaced by the glass-slippered princesses who can discuss fluid balance with the resident but has never gotten the knack of the wrinkle-proof bed.

She is the middle Ms., the mix master who keeps aides and orderlies in circulation (if nothing else) and massages more egos than weary muscles. She is so far removed from patient care she couldn't tell a commode from an Eames chair. Her nail polish is unstained with cocoa butter and she could no more give an effective douche than a painless needle.

The trouble begins with the student nurse, who is now more student than nurse. She is taught evolution and the Rh factor, can hold a conversation better than the fevered hand, and can feel doctor power better than the racing pulse. Once a week this student emerges from the college classroom, doffs her fringed jeans and T-shirt and gets all dressed up in starched miniskirt, brassiere and all. From nine to five she sashays around on the hospital floor learning about orders, forms, reports, staff meetings, and who're the most eligible interns around. In between classes in anthropology and Russian folklore she is whisked through a training in operating rooms, delivery rooms, and nursery, as if being exposed to X rays.

Come Back Cinderella Wherever You Are

She looks down on the old-timer who got her experience on the wards night after night, learning the art of comforting, cleaning, and caring. After all, what does she have in common with a woman who can't discuss the history of transactional analysis, arrange flowers, or write reports? Her business is not the problem of the sick and the infirm lying in rumpled washboard beds an Indian fakir couldn't sleep on. That's not for this breed of cat.

But when our Lady of Lords finally dances the last one at the prom she begins to work on the floors at forty dollars a day, learning on the job to measure the contents of a urinal and getting acquainted with an enema bag. Regardless of whether she can make a bed —she can make an intern. It's found she has a 42 percent better chance than her sister of yesteryear to bag an M.D. till death do they part.

The handwriting is on the wall. We are privy to the passing of that once true sister of charity, the ultimate human empathizer—and there goes the hospital with her. The patient is dead (or still waiting), long live the modern nurse.

Cybernetic Dietetics

Another sign of the times is the so-called hospital diet. Patients have complained about this since the pesthouses of the first crusade. They still complain but it's different now—complaints are expected, almost desired. Hospital culinary success is now measured in nausea units. The food is no longer prepared for the palate but for the disease; it isn't cooked, it's concocted. Graduate dieticians are hired for the express purpose of getting rid of any semblance of taste and they do a remarkable job.

Hospital chefs now get their training in an organic chemistry lab—not among the copper pots and pans but among Pyrex test tubes and beakers. They not only cater to the distorted tastes of the ill—but to each specific symptom. There's a bitter bite for the jaundiced, a sour tang for the ulcered and even a metallic tartness for premenstrual tension. When they burn a chop to a dry crisp, it's to take the strain off those ailing taste buds. Assistant chefs specialize in making sure that everything animal or vegetable is not only devoid of the slightest taste or condiment but must have the consistency of dry cardboard before it passes muster for the cardiac. Hospital food is no longer that hit-and-miss catering to taste and pleasure. It's all for the patient whether he likes it or not, or even whether he eats it or not—if he doesn't want to get well, that's his business.

A House Is Not a (Nursing) Home

There are hospitals for progress and hospitals more or less for patients. There is one other, however, that is for neither. The chip off that old hospital block— the blackest of black sheep is the nursing home. It may not treat anything at all but nursing homes can hardly be as bad as everyone paints them—or as a senate report asserts "number one on the list of unsafe places to live." How could this be when they're serviced, supervised, and even owned by physicians? Sure they're criticized by their more legitimate cousins as flophouses, but this is probably just professional jealousy.

Unlike their fancy cousins, they not only don't run deficits but show handsome profits. They're one of the fastest growing businesses in the United States with almost a billion dollars a year going through the till in New York alone. Who can knock that in bankruptcy city.

There are no doubt pluses and minuses to the nursing home boom, it's just that the minuses bury the pluses. To begin with, they're a contradiction in terms. If these homes nurse anything, it's a profit. As for being a home, the famous madam Polly Adler's house was more a home and cleaner, not so costly, and with less chance of catching disease.

They Shoot Horses Don't They?

If a nation is known by the way it treats its elderly, the United States must rank somewhere near Chad. The elderly get a better deal with the Sioux Indians who put their senior citizens out in the forest to gently pass away. It's mostly government money that supports five thousand or so nursing homes, well heeled at thirty to forty dollars a day (the privately owned go more than ninety dollars). The government will brook no negligence or incompetence with its aged wards. Only licensed M.D.s can supervise the bed sores, malnutrition, and dehydration that are acquired in these homes.

HEW even tried to get the doctor to stop off long enough to write a note for each visit but the doctors objected. They admitted that when they drop in it's hurried, but what can old people expect for free? Is it their duty to supervise the winos and skid rowers who give the elderly their tender loving care but skip meals, medications, and linen changes?

The AMA was up in arms at this lack of trust in the doctor and they beat the rap. So now doctors, as before, can chalk up as many visits as they think a senile eighty-year-old can't recall. Some physicians, whether they see the patient or not, are known to make upward of a hundred thousand a year or nursing home patients—frequently by telephone. Others are ultra-conscientious, seeing forty patients an hour. Some doctors who live in the nursing home neighborhood see patients coming and going—on their way to and from lunch.

No doubt doctors have always been dedicated to the aged. Since Medicare pays they've taken a renewed and more vital interest. Many of them are so interested in the plight of the elderly they'll tip off the nursing home on the sick ones they have in the hospital and advise the family on their rights of riddance.

Finder's fees are paid to special hospital watchers (and doctors, too) who cull patients' charts for the best old bodies that are none too troublesome, none too sick, and none too senile.

Every Day Is Christmas
With Medi(caid or care)

From the records of congressional hearings, nursing homes must be run by either remote control or a phantom. It's always someone else who is to blame for everything. But none were more remotely controlled or managed in a more ghostly (if ghastly) way than those hundred or more run by the pious Mr. Bergman all over New York and New Jersey. Bergman had the government paying for practically everything, including the smoke treatment wafted in from the factories across the street. It's alleged that every podiatrist, hairdresser, or masseuse was a specialist getting Medicaid fees.

The unions, the Catholic, Jewish, and Protestant charities are also in on this action, not too much different from Mr. Bergman, except that by dint of their religious and parochial nature they have more feeling for their own people so they may charge a few thousand extra as a sort of matriculation fee. In contrast to the inefficient hospitals, all of these places are gold mines. They have long waiting lists, a handsome turnover, and an even better turnunder.

There have been all sorts of allegations made against doctors abusing Medicare and Medicaid in nursing homes. The AMA has officially stated this is pure hearsay. It may be sort of a benign neglect—but certainly not fraud. According to government statistics, the doctors can do much better in Medicare without budging from their office, so why should they bother with crosstown traffic getting to those smelly places? Practically the only specialty not caught billing the elderly in this racket seems to be the pediatrician, but the investigation is not yet complete.

Since city, state, and federal money are involved, the politicians work hand in glove with humanitarians like Bergman and, of course, with the doctors. They help smooth out some of the red tape of payments and monthly percentage increases and political problems of zoning and inspection, so that not one elderly patient misses their "care" at forty dollars per.

What Do They Expect, the Ritz?

But even if you can't eat off the nursing home's floor and meals are sometimes served fourteen hours apart and there are more accidents than on a freeway, these havens of mercy do serve a useful function. First there are few patients who get unhealthily obese in these homes, which cuts down on the incidence of stroke and heart disease (their diet works better than Weight Watchers). Though malnutrition is ever present, it's certainly not because of the size of the portions. Some of the best dietitians feel that potato carbohydrate is not lethal and many a starving Biafran would love to get spuds three times a day, seven days a week.

Besides being a haven for those too senile to complain, the major solace of the nursing home is to the family. It takes the elderly off their hands at no cost and hides them so well that the loving offspring need never feel a twinge of conscience.

Overall, this whole hospital era may just be a passing phase of benign neglect for the sick. But even if the pendulum doesn't swing back to the convenience, comfort, and care of yesteryear, considering the huge number of patients run through these hospitals and homes, the number who have survived is a paean to pure human grit. In the meantime more billions than ever before will be poured into caring for our ailing, young. or old. And between the compassion of the government and the dedication of the physician, may the Lord have mercy on our souls.

20

Sacred Cows and Sterile Bulls:

The 100-Billion-Dollar Misunderstanding

(The Establishment)

Dr. Faust made a better deal with the devil than the medical practitioners made with their own establishment. Those movers and dupers, in the 100-billion-dollar health kit and kaboodle may have helped create the modern miracle of medicine but in the process the family doctor was relegated to the status of the specialist flunky, equated with the flim-flam artist and the hospitals and nursing homes with half-way houses to Forest Lawn. With everything going wrong from malpractice to the doctor-patient relationship, the establishment can't even take credit for the one bright spot in the doctor's life—money. Most of the sacred cows of their hierarchy even fought off the mother lode of Medicare for twenty years.

Though one hears of "organized medicine" there could be no more chaotic bunch than the master minds of the healing art. Those who roam and rule these green pastures and have made American Medicine the shiny brights in the world health game are among the loosest bag of doers and shakers Nader ever exposed. Though spoken of in the same reverent breath as the military-industrial complex or the National Rifle Association, one couldn't imagine them agreeing on a choice for corresponding secretary, much less Medicare work. They may have as much clout in congress as the AFL-CIO lobbyists, but they don't even have an address much less a fancy one like their fellow lobbyists the milk producers. But loose or not they are no nickel and dime outfit. In their way and in their own good time things get done—if not for the patient or practitioner, at least for themselves.

They operate only at the highest level (the oval office included) and naturally have little time for the ordinary doctor and his problems. When they're competing with the Soviets to see who can put the first cancer cure on the map, beating the Chinese to the punch with a medical school in Somaliland or upping the NIH budget another billion, how can they be bothered with ethics, doctor-patient relations—or even malpractice. As for the lame and the halt that's for doctors and nurses who have the leisure and the mentality to dawdle with sickness and patients. It's the Indians not the chiefs who must worry with a mother who can't get a doctor for her kid in Harlem or the elderly in their nursing home ghettos.

But regardless of how it affects the physician and his practice the Mary Laskers, the Teddy Kennedys, AID, and AMA and the AHA (American Hospital Association), the American College of Surgeons (or the American College of practically anything else), the Nobel laureates, and all the president's doctors know that health is much too important to be left in the hands of practicing doctors.

The Healer Wheelers

The establishment brotherhood crosses national boundaries as naturally as a surgeon crosses an intern's picket line on the way to the OR. Like the Cabots and the Lodges, the Knowleses of the Rockefeller talk only to the Barbara Castles of London; the Mathews of HEW dine only with the Candaus of WHO, and the

Irving Coopers of Parkinson's disease fame tennis only
with the transplantation Barnards. The health establishment is a blood brotherhood known by the company it
keeps, and these moguls need no oath or ritual as they
work hand in glove with and for each other—if medicine benefits in the process, all to the good.

Though they deal in the merciful field of the sick
and dying, they are wise in the ways of Wall Street—
and are as Machiavellian as a Cook County precinct
captain in getting their fair share of the loot. Their
empires are far-flung and their decisions world-shaking:
from who will be the head of the National Institutes
of Health to which honorary degree will go to whom,
which congressman gets the campaign funds from
AMPAC (the political arm of the AMA) and whether
Medicare fees can be hiked a bit for the suffering specialist. Their lives are busy lining up votes to nominate
their favorite for a Nobel laureate and scrambling for
the seat next to Frank Sinatra at a White House dinner
for the President of Burundi.

Though a loose little island, their world is again
split down the middle. The good guys are on one side
(the liberal, Medicare, Medicaid doers); and those
with the black hats (the conservative, AMA shakers)
on the other. Though as hostile as two surgeons at a
bar mitzvah, they close ranks like a pack of baboons
when threatened—or when it's appropriations time on
the Potomac. They also agglomerate overnight on more
relaxed occasions such as the Heart Association Ball or
a White House signing of a health bill.

When called upon, these celebrities rise and shine,
at the drop of a congressional hearing, prepared statements in hand for the front page and the seven-o'clock
broadcast. Though all have their particular *babies,* if
they get enough press and it doesn't rob their own pet
projects of funds, they'll perform like trained myna
birds for just about any medical cause. Dr. Howard
Rusk has attended more committee hearings on more

diseases far afield from   physical rehabilitation than Ralph Nader has for consumerism.

It's not that they aren't self-serving, their social and political health takes a back seat to no disease. Individually they may receive some small honors like the Nobel prize or the Freedom Medal; some publicity, like a profile in *The New Yorker;* or some little power like an appointment to Assistant Secretary for Health. Still some of this could hardly repay them for the time and effort they put in at banquets, international conventions, fund-raising or fancy dress balls. Who can put a price on getting a congressman's wife admitted to the National Institute of Mental Health or getting a campaign manager's child with a C average into a medical school?

Today the big cancer, heart, and mental health money comes from the government, so if any cancer, heart, or health senator helps put through a bill for a few hundred million for one of Mary Lasker's babies, the National Institute of Health, why shouldn't she throw a fund-raiser for them at campaign time? When John Fogarty of Rhode Island was alive and controlled the congressional purse strings for health, he was a bigger potentate than the Aga Khan and the health fussbudgets weren't allowed to forget it every other November. And AMPAC plays big money politics with the worst of them. Today Teddy Kennedy, Senate Health Sub-Committee chairman, is high man on the medical totem with his national health insurance scheme.

Cancer Can Be Fun.

Like the profession itself, it even pays for the establishment to specialize. Hubert Humphrey knows as much about retardees as the chief of the National

Institute of Mental Health; Bernard Baruch was the cripple's man of the world; Mary Lasker (she even has her own little Nobel type Lasker prize) specialized in cardiology, and almost single-handedly got the first National Heart Institute going. She has now switched —anyone who wants anything in cancer had better reckon with her (Mary is a shaker among shakers and what Mary wants, Mary gets—at least when the Democrats are in).

Cancer is a typical example of the fruits of specialization. If a shaker can't make a name for himself in this he'd better return to the bush league of Tay-Sachs disease or epilepsy. Cancer has pizzazz, box office, and glamour, and in actual dollars and prestige, even heart and mental can't hold a candle to it. It's a health dodge with a future and everybody who's anybody is jumping in, especially politicians. (Who votes against a cure for cancer?)

Just a few years back, a Harvard cancer specialist and nineteen others came up with a billion-dollar idea —a new cancer institute to buy an overnight cure for this "dread disease" (to Madison Avenue cancer is always a "dread disease," as if stroke, multiple sclerosis, and nephritis can be shaken off like a runny nose). Though we already have a well endowed Cancer Institute, this formidable twenty had the great American dream of finishing it off like polio which coincidently get them each six more lines in *Who's Who* and more kudos for Harvard. So with the name (Harvard) and the game (money) on the line, the juggernaut for a new institute was cranked up with a press campaign that made Mao's propaganda look like a high school mimeograph operation. Congressional hearings were set and the grapevine alerted with the networks grinding away. All the best people in or out of cancer said their prepared piece (written by the best cancer hacks) and all the cancer senators and congressmen (mostly democratic good guys) got a lot of mileage out of it. They never got their institute (thanks to Nixon) but

they did get a hundred million dollars a year extra for
their efforts (now up to eight hundred million). This
can't guarantee the luck or the brains necessary for a
breakthrough, but will put some of the "right" unem-
ployed professors and researchers from the right institutions back at the public trough.

As a specialization cancer has shown its clout in
creating professional fiefdoms and jobs along with a
bevy of feature stories. But cancer can also be fun
with its luncheons, theater parties, and fund-raising
luaus. Besides which the Cancer Society, the Damon
Runyon Fund, and other such keep droves of women
from Hagerstown to Park Avenue off the streets and
out of trouble with hours and hours of planning for
balls and theater parties. Motivated by the humanitarian desire of showing off their latest Givenchy they'll
buy ten-gallon coffee urns for every lab in the country.
There is only one built-in risk here; what will they all
do if a cure comes out of it? Considering how easily
the March of Dimes conglomerate shifted gears after
the polio vaccine, it should pose no problem.

In any event, this is how the collective establishment
gets its way. And as long as a doctor's life, fee schedule, leisure and pension plans are ultimately run by
others besides his wife, his mistress, or his office nurse,
he should know something about those who comprise
the establishment.

The AMA—the American Medical Anathema

First and foremost is the medical left's big bogeyman—the AMA. It is truly the only well organized
power group that stands out in this mass of disorganiza-
tion. Talk about medical clout, the white-hat Democratic do-gooders may be out front and on top but the
old whipping boy, the AMA, though down, is hardly

out. Its rolls may have shrunk; it is being audited for
a possible liability of twenty-one million by the IRS;
investigated for secretly collaborating with the drug
industry on drug price controls; and it picked mostly
congressional losers in the 1974 elections—but don't
sell it short. Doctors can rave and rant about that
august body but let no one say it didn't put the M.D.
in the driver's seat. It may be to the right of the Ku
Klux Klan and have shown little concern about the
delivery of medical care to the poor and disenfranch-
ised, but it has certainly delivered the loot to every
practicing doctor for the past twenty-five years. Even
practitioners that don't belong know who takes care
of them when the fur flies.

When it comes to politics they're no white knights—
witness AMPAC (American Medical Political Action
Committee). They've been against the twentieth century ever since the nineteenth and have been against
every Democratic president since Roosevelt. If George
Wallace goes or if Barry or Ronald are revived, they'll
be there with the boodle. They put the pressure on
through their 168,000 precinct workers who see voters
six hundred million times a year. At one point they
even elected their own type of president, Dr. Anis (the
spelling is correct or incorrect according to your per-
spective and leaning), more conservative than John
Birch.

The AMA isn't always right (as the Democrats are
not loath to point out) but this Dr. Anis, who led the
good fight against Medicare as the sure road to socialized medicine and Communism, pulled the biggest
bungle of the AMA's long and distinguished financial
career. He—like so many others—hadn't the faintest
idea that Medicare was really a license to steal. The
AMA fought this tooth and nail from Truman to
L.B.J. and now that it's arrived it turns out to be a
fiscal miracle that makes General Motors look like
the corner grocer. Every doctor past the age of seventy
should sue the AMA for the billions in windfall he

could have grabbed had it accepted Medicare ten years earlier. Now this governing body is leary about National Health Insurance. But in its beady eyes there lurks the look of a Shylock stumbling onto another pot of gold.

Power Pals

When it comes to individual M.D.s in the power business, most would be lost without their lay patrons —and their patrons without them. Where would that Missourian Dr. Howard Rusk be (now a Bellevue professor with his own Rehabilitation Institute) if he hadn't jockeyed himself into meeting Sulzberger of the *Times* or that advisor to presidents, Bernard Baruch, on his favorite park bench. One would question whether Luther Terry, Senator Lister Hill's godson, became surgeon general of the U.S. in simple professional competition with his peers. Philip Lee, the son of a doctor, with direct power lines to Mary Lasker and Howard Rusk, got to be the first Assistant Secretary of Health in the department of HEW. There also is the golden boy of New York, Dr. Irving Cooper, the brain freezer who has more beautiful people patrons in and out of his chauffeured Rolls Royce than even handsome six-foot Denton Cooley, the M.D. with the mostest hostesses in Houston. And then there is Dr. William Walsh whose Jackie O. connection makes his *Good Ship Hope* Ball a winner every year.

All the President's Doctors

Always high on the roost in the medical hen house (with a medical patron second to none) but frequently not hip enough to know what to do with it, are All the

President's Doctors. Most of them come free from the military (as well they should) and maybe they do well in a naval battle but some couldn't treat their way out of a hangnail epidemic. But that isn't important. When the White House doctor runs into something other than an ailment a junior lifesaver could take care of, he'll go for outside help—as was done with Ike, L.B.J., and R.M.N. Some of those consultants, like Dr. Max Jacobson (Dr. Feelgood) with his "upper" injections for the Strangelove set, could get through to the Oval Office quicker than the secretary of state. It's no small potatoes to have the president's ear, or at least his buttock, almost daily.

When the new doctor at 1600 Pennsylvania Avenue opens up shop the health vultures move in before he's given the president his first dose of Librium. No matter which party is in, he is included at every establishment head table, wined and dined by the AMA, the drug houses, and the health bureaucracy. He is actually used more than included.

Secretary of the State of Health

One of the great power players in the establishment today is Dr. John Knowles, an Elliot Richardson protégé.

He is not only medically political but politically political and was once chosen to be the lieutenant governor of Massachusetts on a ticket that unluckily (or luckily) for him didn't materialize. After a shot at assistant secretary of health which Nixon deflected, he wound up as admiral of the Rockefeller Flagship, the foundation which is richer, more prestigious and powerful than many governments. As one of the pillars of the foundation arm of the establishment, John Knowles hasn't had much time to see patients since his intern stint, but he can tell nations like Taiwan or Korea not only what they should eat but how many children they should have and which diseases need tackling. His decisions, along with those of his brothers in arms, from Ford, Milbank, and Johnson to a thousand lesser foundations, determine everything from who'll run the National Heart Institute to how many female medical students should be admitted.

World, Say Ah!

When looking at the big health picture, the World Health Organization (WHO) and its Latin American branch office, the Pan American Health Organization, moves with the best of them. The arts of boondoggling, shifting, backtracking, and procrastinating never reached its apogee until medical machos like Caudau and Horowitz latched onto the UN teat. They make deals for millions of people, parceling out hundreds of millions of dollars of World Bank loans and grants where it will do the most good—for their own offices, their nation, and, if anything's left, for the UN. They offer million-dollar international conferences and malaria programs that can change the face of nations and demand little more than a UN vote or two in exchange. If administrative and travel expenses aren't too heavy and there's not too much pressure to hire twenty more Brazilians or ten more Tanzanians, they may have something left over for at least a few worthy studies where it counts. Talk about medical power, a WHO grant to wipe out the tropical disease yaws put Papa Doc and his family in charge of Haiti for life.

Of Hole Cloth

Though not all of these sacred cows are sacred, some are men not only of the spirit but of the cloth.

They are those doctors and missionaries who by sheer will and publicity made it into the establishment's charmed circle.

Albert Schweitzer was the model of these jungle types, though strangely enough no martyr; he was too stable and smart for that. He lived to see his idea take secular root, first with Dr. Seagraves, the Burma surgeon who was overthrown and exiled by his own native staff; then with Dr. Larry Mellon, the prodigal son of the Pittsburgh clan who later put up a posh jungle establishment in Haiti; Tom Dooley who founded Medico after discharge from the Navy under peculiar circumstances (he's recently been proposed for sainthood) and even Jackie Kennedy's obstetrician, William Walsh, with the biggest boondoggle of them all, the *Good Ship Hope* (which cost the U.S. government and the beautiful people about five thousand dollars for every case of jungle rot cured). Dozens of these merciful healing missions tugged at the heart and purse strings of the American people through churches, synagogues, and the *Mike Douglas Show,* examples of medical altruism at its best. Many of these part-time messiahs would spend nine or ten months of sacrifice and martyrdom at the Plaza and the "21," then, put their hair shirts back on to return to their beloved jungle for a month or six weeks to treat the betel-chewing natives.

But the bloom came off the rose when a black woman in Harlem asked, "How come they go twelve thousand miles out to the jungle when they wouldn't come around the corner for my kid with a temperature of 106?"

Medical Mendicants

The Mayos from Minnesota, the Menningers from Kansas, the Criles from Cleveland, the Lovelaces from

New Mexico, plus the golden-tower professors from Harvard and Yale must be included in any listing of "our crowd." They not only have tentacles into the NIH treasury but their graduates have hooks into the best and the biggest grants and endowments. Of the 300,000 physicians in America, 100,000 of them are deans, chiefs, administrators, and researchers. Holed up in these noble institutions their time goes almost exclusively to thinking up programs and problems to squeeze funds out of the U.S. Treasury.

Without the federal health budget, most of our medical schools would be back to grave robbing and most of the professors would have to go back to seeing patients. As former members in good standing of this club the medical honchos of HEW, AID, and the likes of Dr. James Shannon, who ran his multi-billion dollar NIH like an auld sod clan leader, worked hand in glove with them in a most healthy and wealthy relationship.

Most are more at home in a transatlantic jet than in their own medical school or clinic offices, going not to where diseases are, but where the action is. In the '50s they inspected the developing nations from the vantage point of the Copacabana, New Delhi, or even London. In the '60s they studied the medical experiences of the Eastern bloc countries from the Bolshoi in Moscow to the Hermitage in Leningrad. Though the big problem of the '70s is the delivery of medical care to some fifty million Americans who can't get a doctor, these guiding lights of the profession are now doing their China thing.

The Ignoble Laureates

Then there are the darlings of the establishment and a power in their own right, the Nobel laureates. As every medical school and hospital knows one laureate is worth a thousand grants. These medical celebs were either frustrated doctors who became laboratory recluses when they couldn't get into a medical school or doctors who couldn't stand people. After being cooped up for twenty years in their malodorous laboratory without being invited down to the cafeteria for a tuna on rye, they are suddenly the toast of the medical town, out of their old sneakers and into lunches at the Côte Basque, people hanging on their every medical or nonmedical word. Overnight they become TV authorities on subjects they have little knowledge about, like Linus Pauling with the common cold, Shockley on race relations, and the beaded hippy laureate George Wald on the psychological and sociologic implications of the lost foreskin. As recent history has shown, even the laureates of the DNA scandal weren't too noble.

If the Past is Prologue—the Future Looks Profitable

So doctors and nurses, wherever you are—these are your leaders. Take them as they are, for though a motley crew, there is no truer reflection of the mind and mores of medicine in the marketplace.

Now after a hundred years of leading you to the promised land there are signs the sacred cows may take it all back. For slowly but surely they are guiding you wealthy fortunates down the garden path to that bogeyman in every red blooded M.D.s nightmare—National Health Insurance (socialized medicine). And the very best of you—the AMA—are going along. Though it's only natural if the government shells out billions and billions of dollars each year that minor annoyances would be expected—but take over the whole bag? What will happen to the medical free enterprise system —and your incomes? Will house calls come back, will diet doctors and cosmetic surgeons disappear, will millions of tonsillectomies go undone and will the $5,000 operation be a thing of the past? Hardly!

If past experience has taught us anything, it's never underestimate the resourcefulness of the rank and file physician. History is with him. No matter what the system will be those self-same physicians who've given us the nursing home problem, made a guaranteed annual income out of Medicaid, thrown Medicare into virtual bankruptcy, and almost alone have seen to it that Blue Cross premiums rise at least 20 percent or so a year will stand shoulder to shoulder for the common weal. They'll never allow the manner of life to which they have become accustomed to perish from these shores.